How to Draw Awesome Figures
By Neil Fontaine

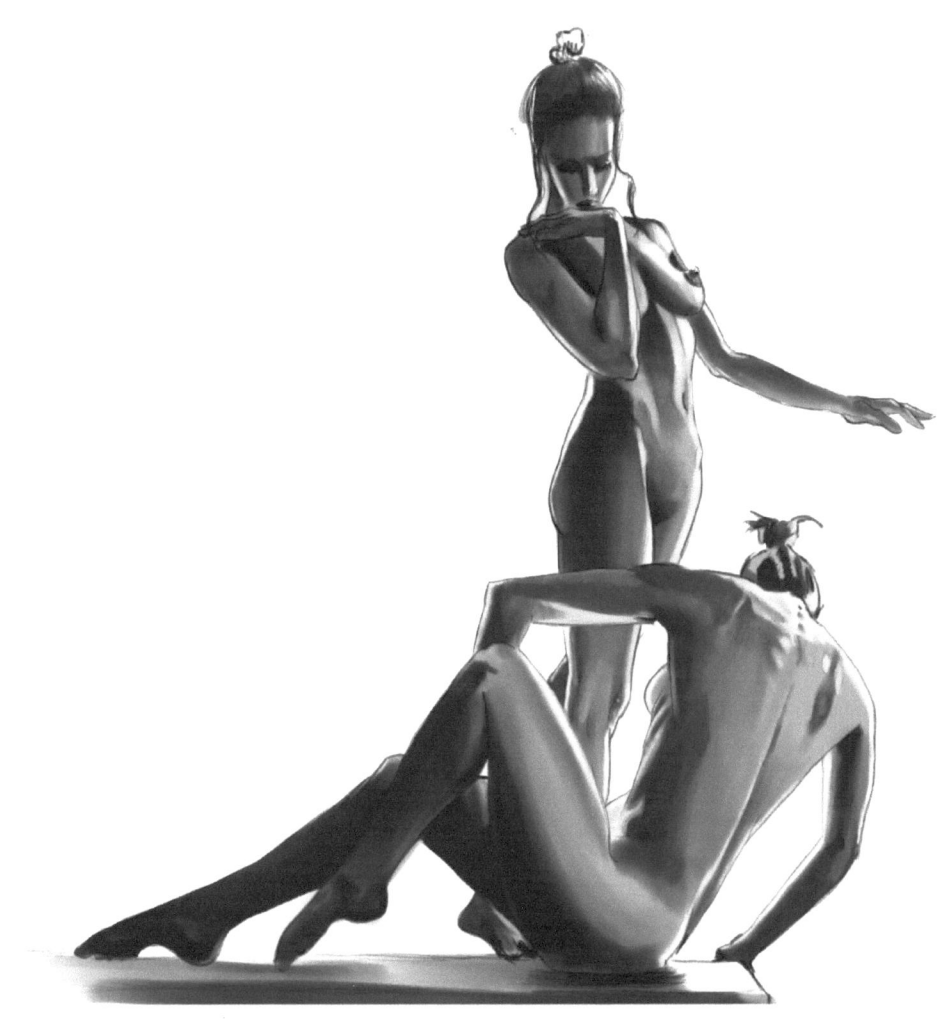

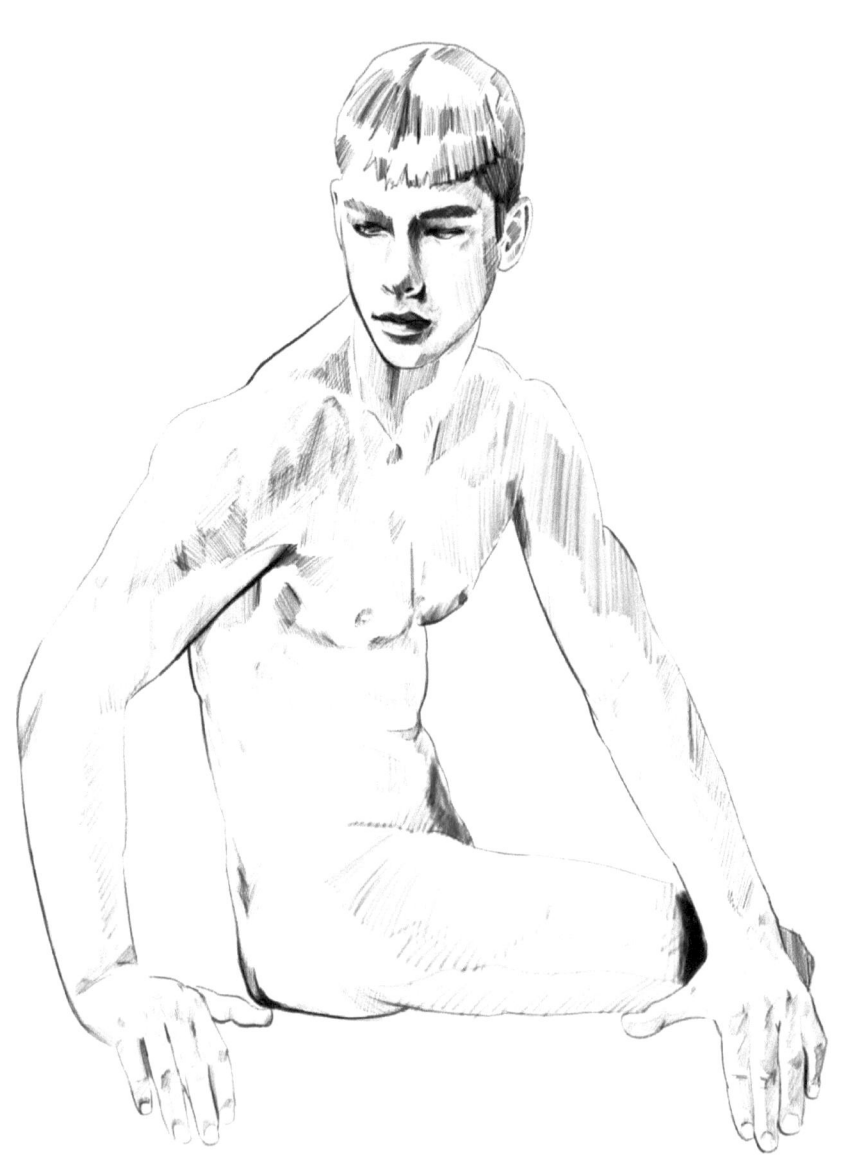

Table of Contents

Introduction

Hi, I'm Neil Fontaine, the art instructor at http://masterpaintingnow.com and the top art instructor at Udemy. I studied art in San Jose, California as well as did a lot of personal study. I then went on to teach how to draw and have been doing so since 2006. (You can access my full video courses by clicking here. They are only $30 for full courses and often on sale for under $15.)

During this time, I have developed a simple-to-learn system for drawing the human figure. Once learned, you will draw people quickly and easily. So, if you want to draw amazing figures for your concept art characters and comic characters, then read this book.

What you will and will not learn

To keep this book affordable and on point, we're going to focus mainly on drawing the figure, both male and female. We will not go into detail about the face, poses, character design, etc. All that knowledge is necessary to creating great characters, but first, and most importantly, we need to learn to draw the figure properly.

The focus of this book is to get you drawing the human figure from your imagination. To do that, you need to not only learn the basic figure, but you will need to learn some anatomy, like where muscles attach.

I know, anatomy sounds boring and too hard to learn, but I break it down in a simple way that anyone can understand. On top of that, I only focus on the muscles and bones that are important to drawing figures from imagination.

I include several reference photos and drawings for you to study and use.

As a quick side note, when I say you need to learn to draw the human figure from imagination, I mean without any references, without looking at anything, not a photo, drawing, or person. This might sound impossible, but believe me it's not. I've done it.

After I achieved this ability to draw the human figure completely from imagination, I found a new bliss in drawing, one I never felt before. I found drawing exciting again.

How to read this kindle book.

Before every picture, I will give you important information about the image. Please read everything. If you don't, then you are missing the whole point of the book. I know what you might be thinking. I remember when I first started learning to draw, I just flipped through my drawing books, thinking I would magically learn to draw better by drawing the images in the book.

I didn't read them. I wish I had. Why spend money on a book and not read it?

If I could rewind time, I would read all those drawing books right away. Instead, I didn't, not until much later in life, in my 20's. I had to learn all the fundamentals by actually reading the books.

Don't worry, though. My teaching style is quick and on point, so you will not have to do much reading in order to learn how to draw the human figure for your comics and concept art.

Chapter 1: Proportions

This is probably the most important part of figure drawing to master. If you fail to master the proportions of the figure, then all your figures will look off, no matter how awesome all the details are. Let's look at an example of the same figure, one with proper proportions--the other without. The drawing details are the same, though.

The legs are too short and breast too high on the left image. Also her left arm, our right is too long. These simple proportional mistakes make the figure look off, despite how good the details might be.

So take the time to study this chapter and do the exercises.

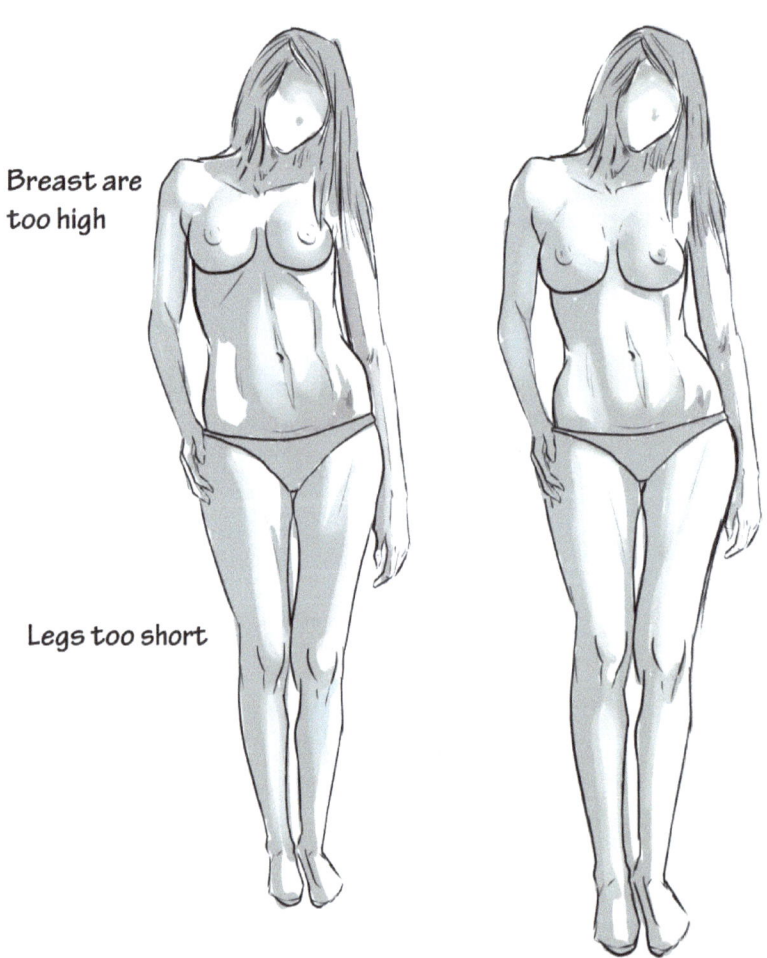

Breast are too high

Legs too short

Professional concept artists and comic artists use the eight headed figure the most, so we will first learn to draw the eight-headed figure. All relative proportions can be based on the eight-headed figure.

We will draw the female by learning her proportions, then we will learn the differences of the male, because If you can draw the female, then you can draw the male.

Draw a line. Divide it in half. Then divide the bottom half in half. The knees will go just above that line.

Divide the top half in half, then divide that half in half again. The top section is where you will draw the head. The width of the head is about half its height. In the top 3rd of the second section, draw the collar bones. This gives you the length of the neck, as you can see in the drawing below.

Next is an easy way to get the length of the rib cage and placement of the belly button. Draw stick arms extending from the edge of the collar bone to the halfway line, which is where the crotch will be. Then divide that arm length in half. The rib cage will reach just below this halfway mark of the arm. It also marks the elbow area of the arm.

Draw simple rectangle shapes for the hand placement. The hand is almost as tall as the head.

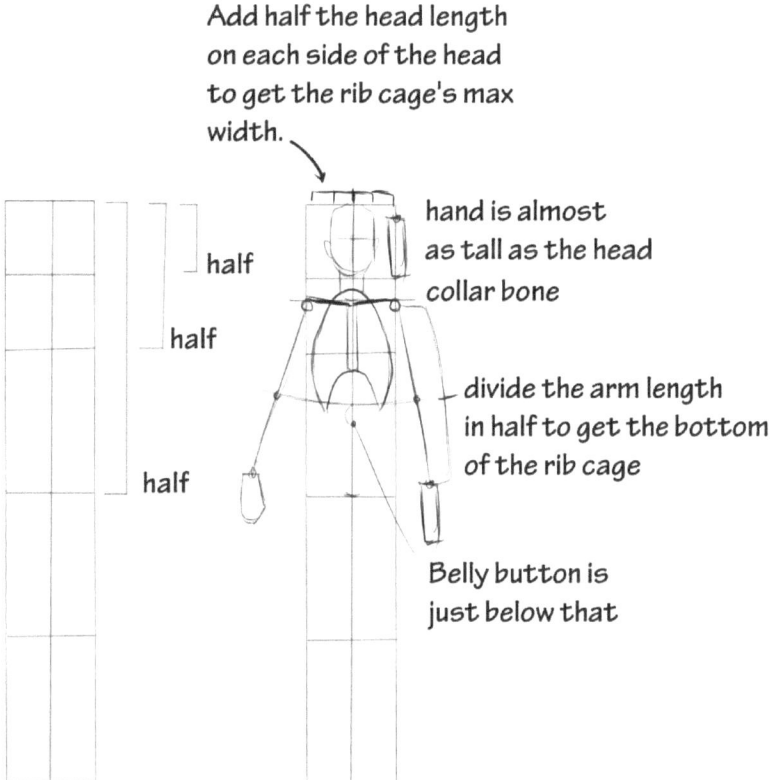

Add half the head length on each side of the head to get the rib cage's max width.

half

half

half

hand is almost as tall as the head

collar bone

divide the arm length in half to get the bottom of the rib cage

Belly button is just below that

Next we will draw the hips and stick-figure leg bones.

When you draw the hips, draw them as a triangle. The height of the triangle goes from the crotch line to just below the bellybutton.

The stick-figure leg bones have an S curve to them. I will show you this is true with a picture of a skeleton. I will also show you an alternative way to draw legs to be a bit longer, which can add sexiness to your female figures.

The most important part of the femur (upper leg bone) is that is comes off the hips at an angle. This makes the widest section of the female figure, which happens to fall at the crotch line.

Be sure to draw the knees above the halfway leg line. Also, the feet take up a third of the lowest section, as you can see in the drawing below.

Draw this stick figure many times until it feels natural to draw it from imagination. This is the most important foundation you need to master. Without this, you will not be able to draw good figures from imagination, and that is a necessary skill as a comic or concept artist.

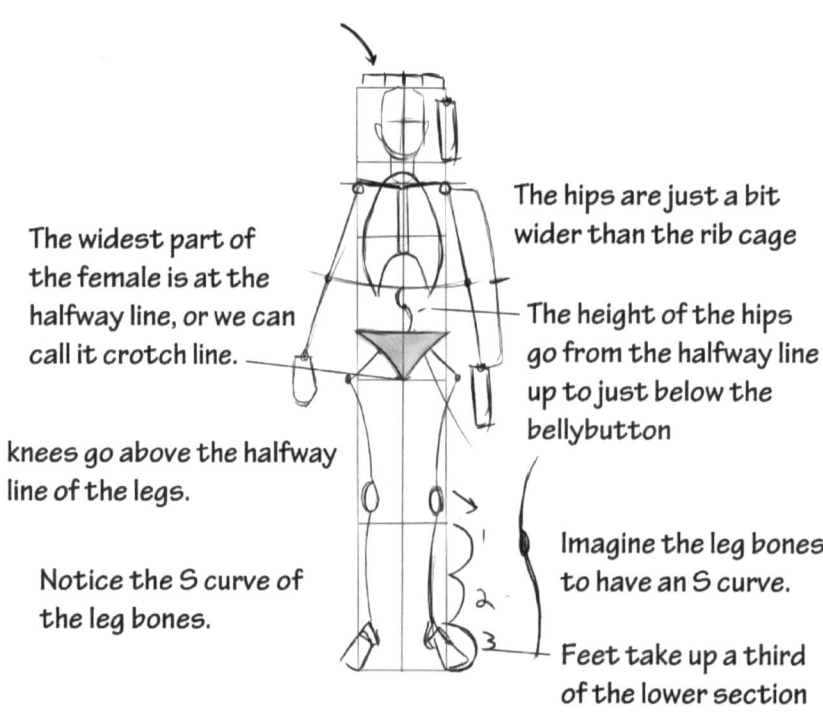

The widest part of the female is at the halfway line, or we can call it crotch line.

knees go above the halfway line of the legs.

Notice the S curve of the leg bones.

The hips are just a bit wider than the rib cage

The height of the hips go from the halfway line up to just below the bellybutton

Imagine the leg bones to have an S curve.

Feet take up a third of the lower section

Here is a picture of the skeleton, so we can see how accurate the stick figure skeleton I taught you represents it.

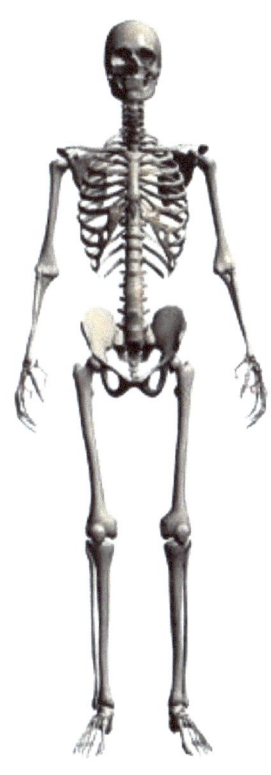

Now you can see how the stick-figure skeleton represents the real skeleton. However, there is no reason to commit to memory the actual skeleton. Only the stick-figure skeleton. The important bones that show through the body, we will go over later. For now, draw the stick-figure skeleton at least 20 times from reference, measuring accurately each time. Only then try to draw it from imagination.

If you fail at drawing it from imagination, then draw it from reference 10 more times before attempting to draw it from imagination again. By imagination, I mean use no references.

Also, be sure to let the information sink in for a day. You will find the next day that you can draw the stick figure much better. It might take a few days or even weeks to master the stick figure, so that you can draw it from imagination without errors. Be patient.

They say in order to be good at something, you must do it a thousand times. Just like playing the piano takes lots of practice, so does drawing. You must draw the stick figure over and over, filling up pages before it will come naturally to you.

Chapter 2: The Mannequin

Once you have mastered the stick figure, the mannequin will be easy to draw. However, if you were lazy with learning to draw the stick figure, then your mannequins will look odd. You might not understand why they don't look that good. It will be because the proportions are off.

Master the stick figure. It is super important.

Now we will learn how to transform a stick figure into a mannequin, and then how to turn a mannequin into a finished drawing, which takes learning some anatomy. That will probably take the longest to learn. But for now, let's just learn the mannequin.

To get the placement of the breasts, divide the ribcage in half. That is the center of the breasts, where the nipples would go. Be sure to draw the breasts oval and not round. Also, be sure to draw them at an angle and not straight down. (You might want to check out the image below, then come back up here and read.)

Draw the neck almost down to the collar bone, then draw to diagonal lines that touch the upper part of the arm. These lines represent the traps, which we will learn later.

At any time, you might need to scroll down to the drawing so to better make sense of the instructions I write above the drawing.

Draw the love handles extending from the top of the triangle to just above her belly button. Be sure to curve them in, but don't touch the ribcage. Now draw small lines to connect the love handles to the ribcage.

When you draw the legs, draw the inside line from the crotch to just past the knee. Draw a basic tapering cylinder that comes to a point. For the outside of the leg, start at the top of the triangle and draw past the knee.

Notice that the outside of the leg is longer than the inside of the leg. Notice also that the femur bone (upper leg bone) presses against the outside of the leg, making this the widest part of the female body. You can actually feel that bone at the edge of your upper thigh.

An important note: The outer side of the leg connects to the same part of the triangle (hip bone) as does the lower part of the love handle.

If you want, you can draw horizontal lines at the hip line and the crotch line, forming a miniskirt.

Not like this 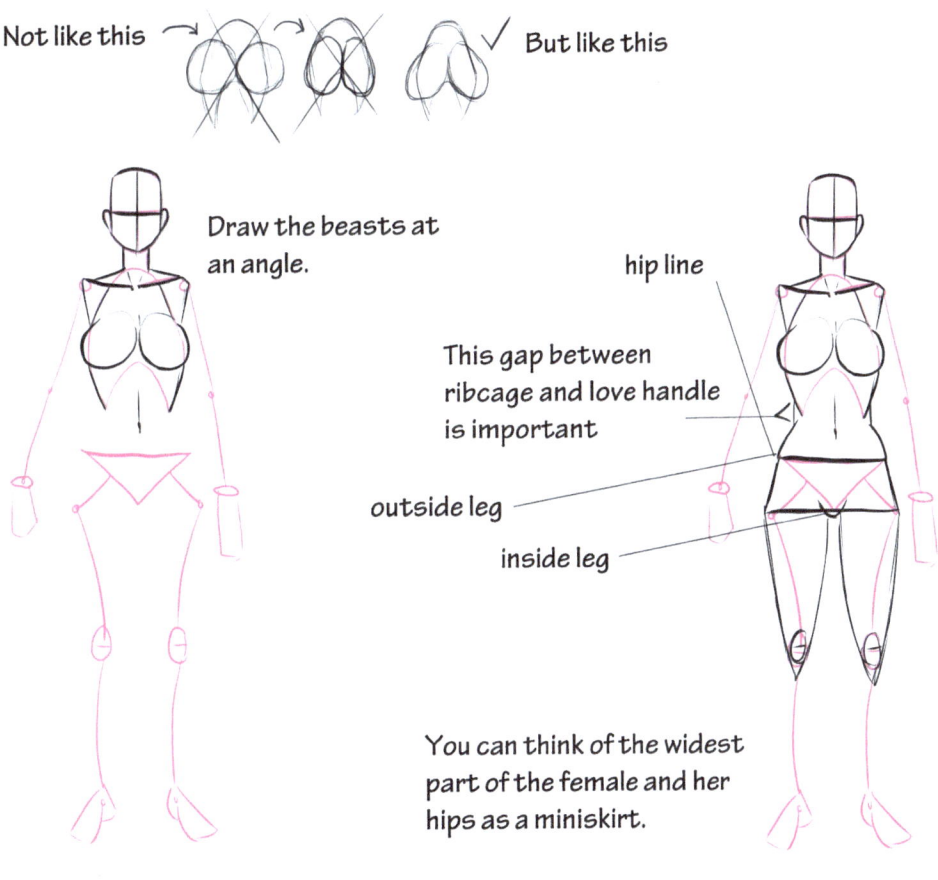 ✓ But like this

Draw the beasts at
an angle.

hip line

This gap between
ribcage and love handle
is important

outside leg

inside leg

You can think of the widest
part of the female and her
hips as a miniskirt.

To finish off the mannequin, simply draw the lower legs as tapered cylinders, down to the ankles, then draw the simplified feet.

To draw the arms, first divide the upper arm in half. The shoulder extends to that halfway mark. Then draw a cylinder to represent the biceps, triceps area.

Then draw another tapered cylinder to represent the forearm. Redrew the basic hand rectangle.

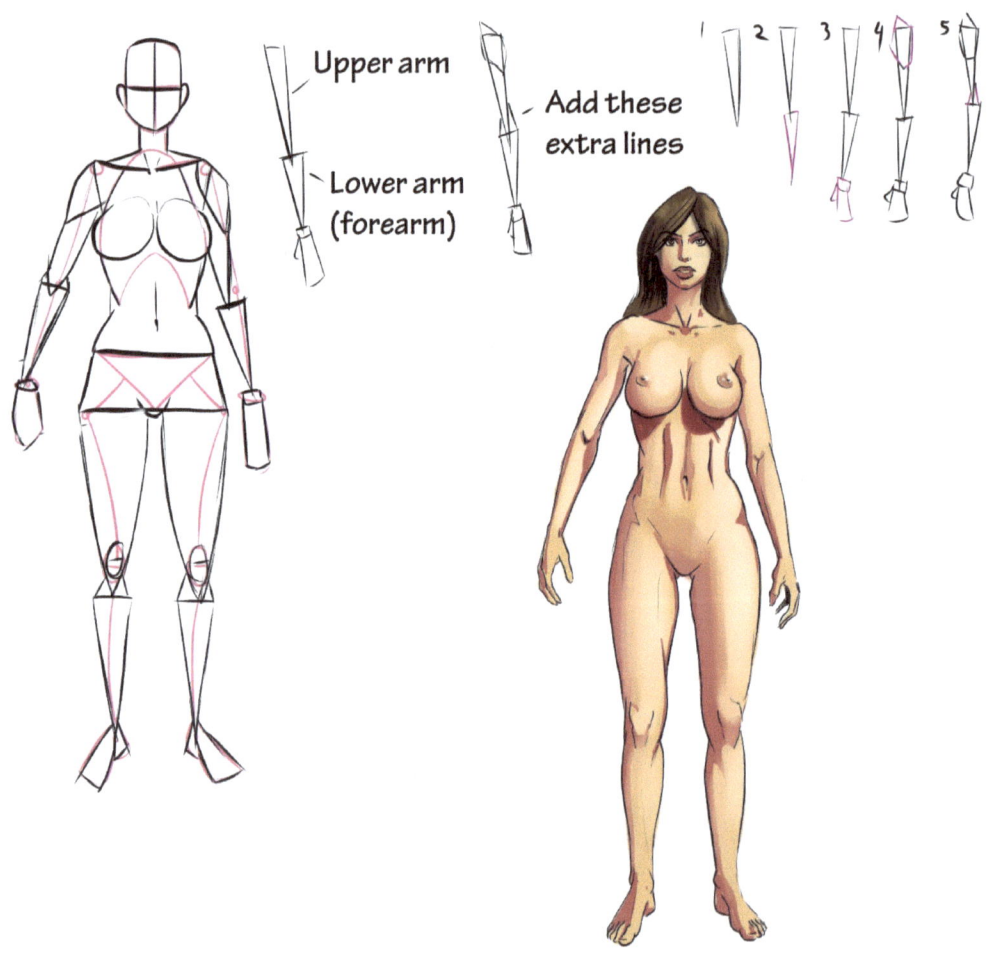

After you master the mannequin, then you can add however much realism you wish by adding in the anatomy. We will learn anatomy a bit later.

Also, we started off with a simple pose to learn the front view basic skeleton and mannequin. We will also keep the poses simple to learn the side view, back view, and ¾ view. All these views are important to learning anatomy, and then later learning how to add coolness to our poses.

However, this book will only briefly talk about gesture drawing, and adding the anatomy onto our cool poses, as that subject deserves a whole book.

Adding interest to the front view

Let's add interest to our front view pose by drawing her leaning her weight on mostly one leg, which pushes the hips up on the side the weight is on. In this case, we will put the weight on her left leg, our right.

Doing so will not change the shape of the hips or ribcage, but will change the angles of them. Her left leg, which is on our right, will push the hips up on our right side, her left.

If her left hip is pushed up then drop her right shoulder

To balance her, draw her collar bones and ripcage at an opposite angle

Because her hips are on an angle and her ripcage on the opposite angle, the center of her collar bones slides over to her right.

Weight pushes up on the hip so draw it at an angle

Her right leg has to bend or come forward, go backward or go to the side.

The side the weight is on gets crunched. The opposite side gets stretched

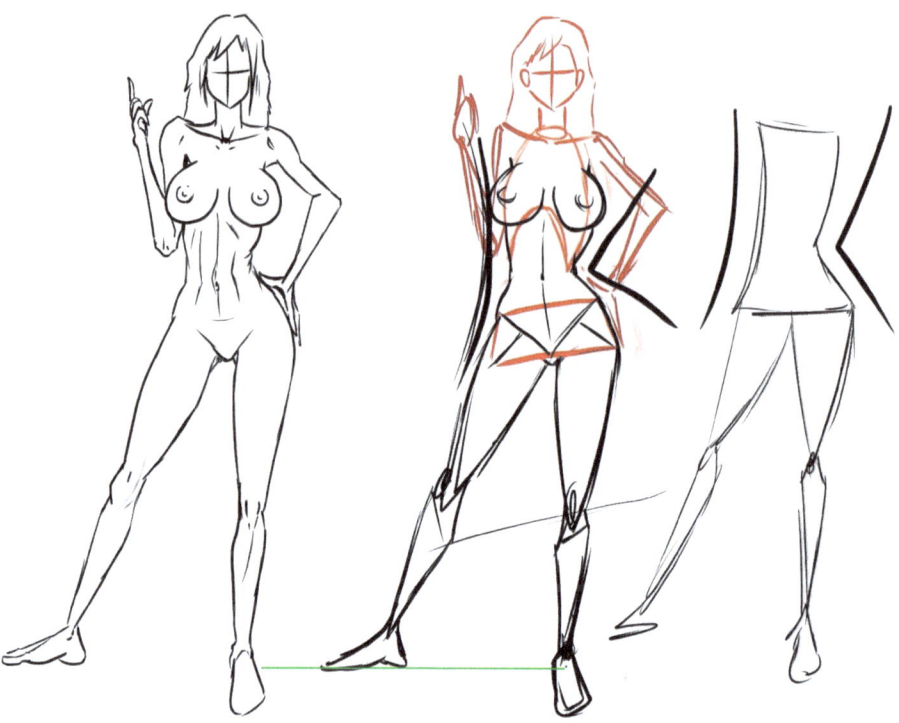

The difference between male and female

To draw a male, we only need to make a few changes to the female skeleton and mannequin. Let's start with the skeleton.

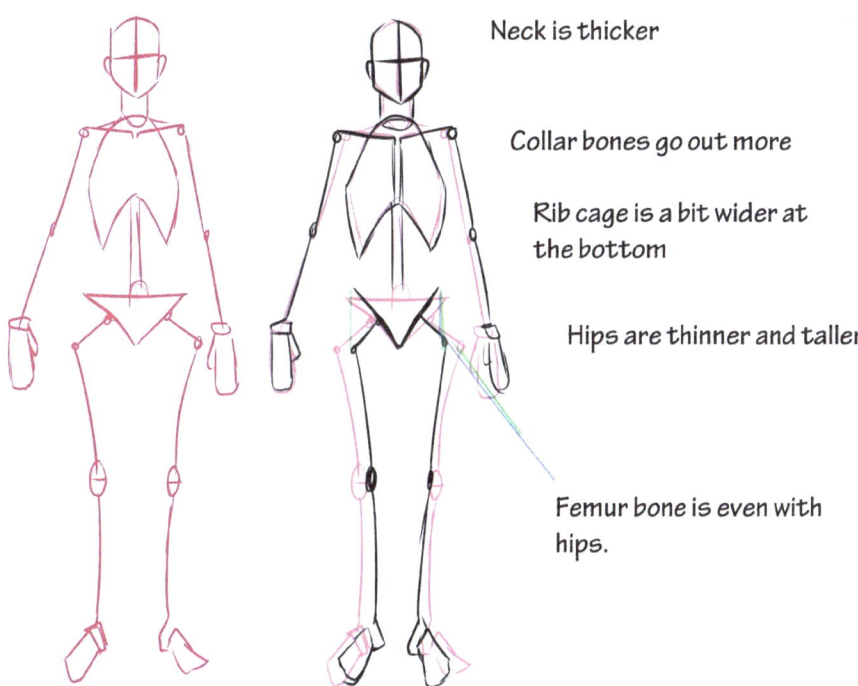

Neck is thicker

Collar bones go out more

Rib cage is a bit wider at the bottom

Hips are thinner and taller

Femur bone is even with hips.

The main things to keep in mind when drawing the male mannequin is the neck is thicker, shoulders are broader, ribcage is thicker, hips are narrower, love handles are shorter, and the legs are thicker.

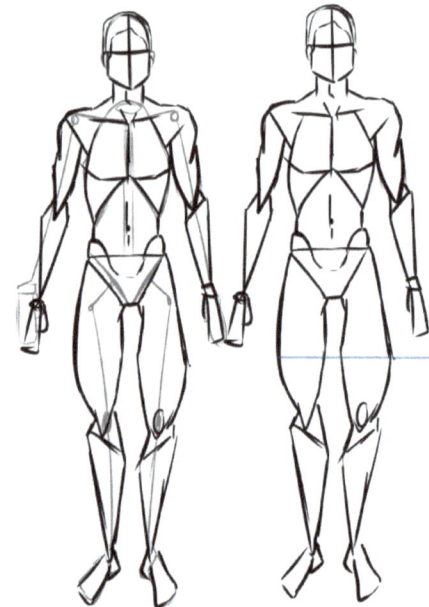

Do the same to the mannequin. Make the neck thicker, ribcage thicker, shoulders broader, hips narrower, love handers shorter, and finally, make the legs thicker.

Thickest part of the legs

For your exercises, draw both the male and the female many times. Fill up pieces of paper, be those pieces of paper digital or traditional. Try drawing different poses from the front view by shifting the weight differently on one leg, or both legs far apart, etc.

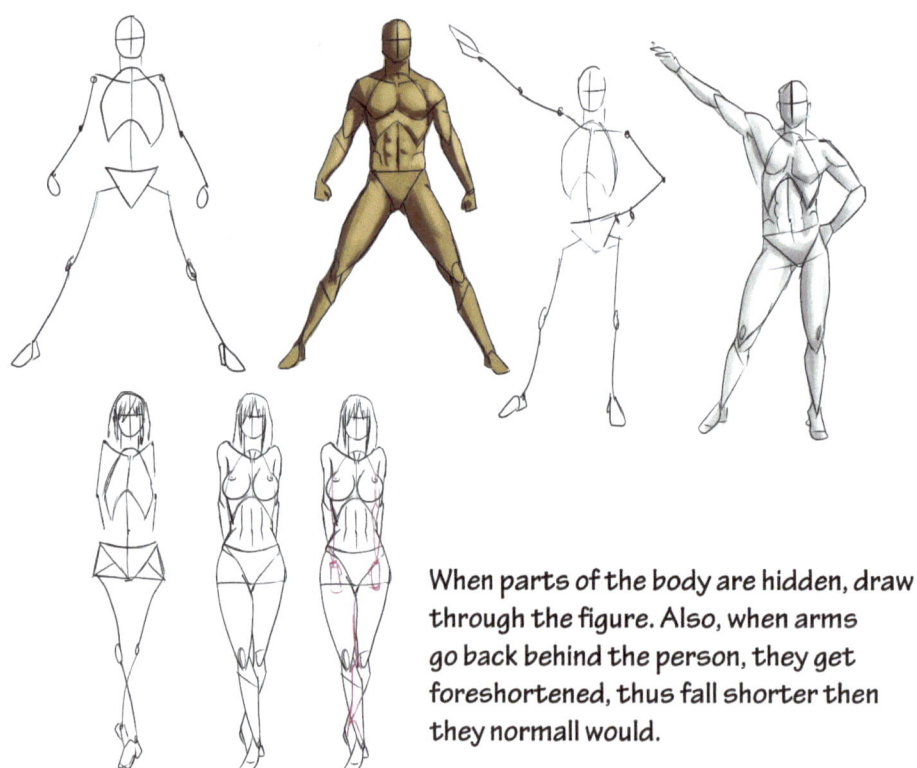

When parts of the body are hidden, draw through the figure. Also, when arms go back behind the person, they get foreshortened, thus fall shorter then they normall would.

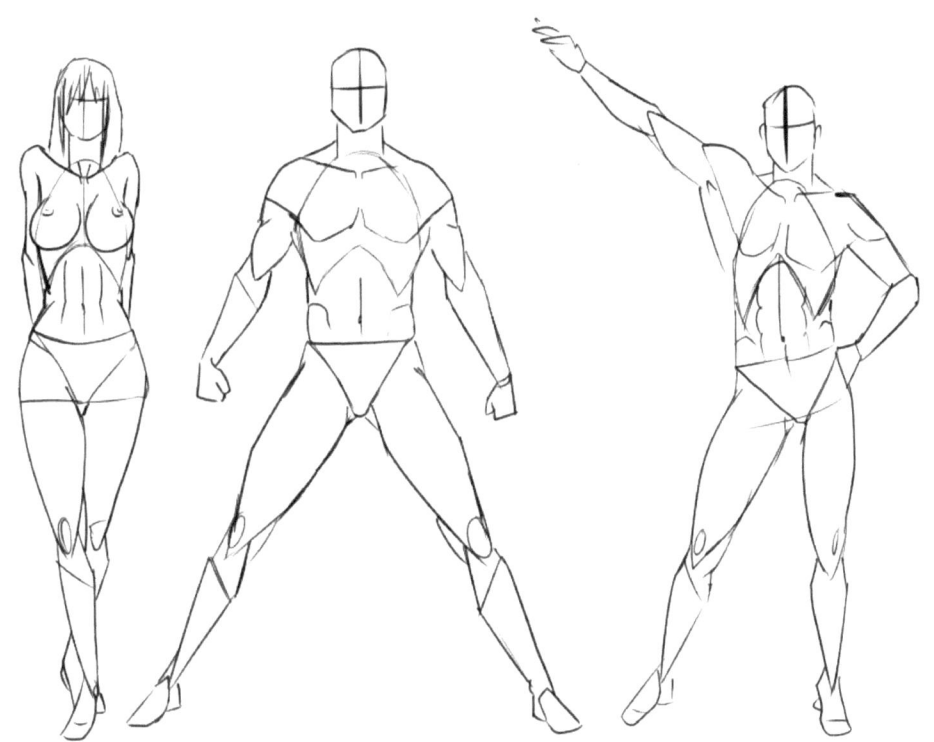

Skeleton and Mannequin back view

The back view is similar to the front view. This shouldn't take you as long to learn as the front view did because you are taking a lot of information you already know from the front view.

Let's start with the skeleton.

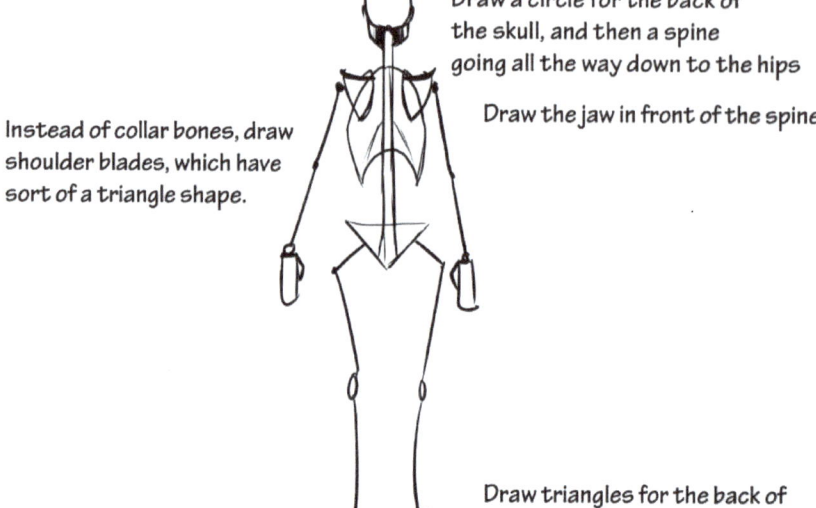

Draw a circle for the back of the skull, and then a spine going all the way down to the hips

Draw the jaw in front of the spine

Instead of collar bones, draw shoulder blades, which have sort of a triangle shape.

Draw triangles for the back of the feet.

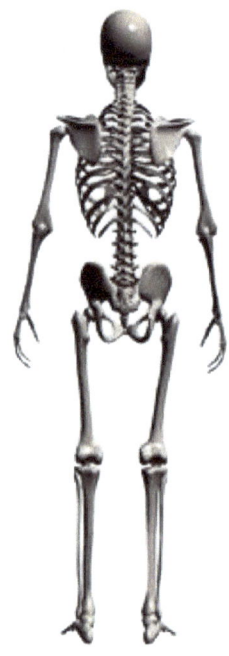

Backside mannequin

Learning the backside skeleton should be easy. However, the backside mannequin might take a bit longer to learn because there is more new information.

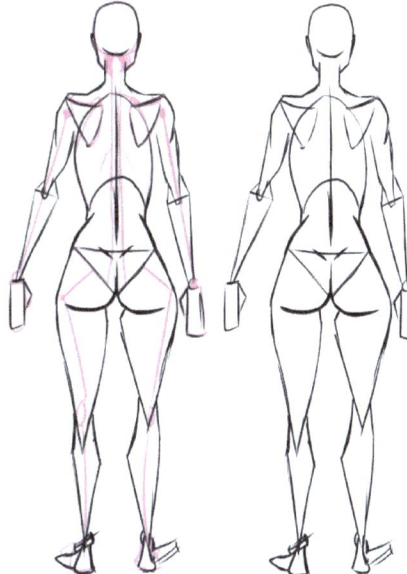

Still draw the shoulder blades, rib cage, and triangle for the hips.

For the back of the arms, change the shape a bit to account for the elbows.

From the backside, the love handles extend a bit higher, and more toward the center of the body.

The bottom of the buttocks extend a bit lower then the crotch. This is important.

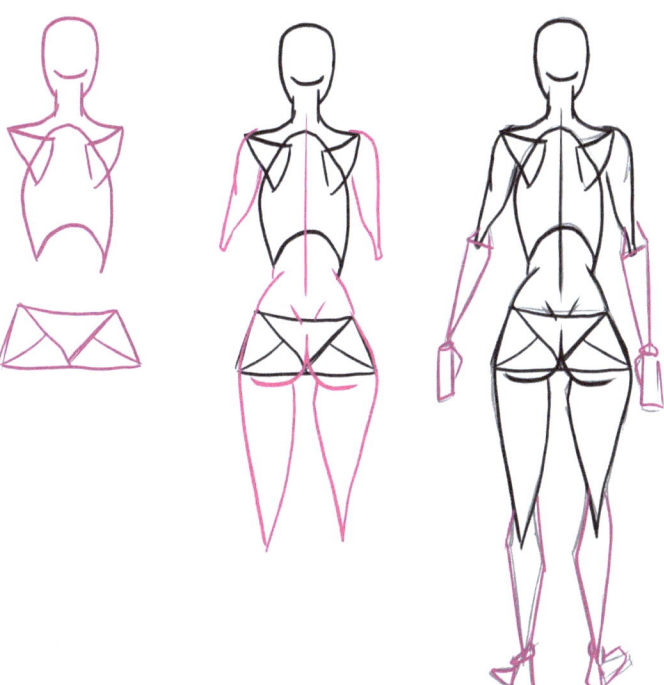

When you draw the male stick-figure skeleton and the mannequin from the back side, draw them with the same differences we learned from the front view. The neck is thicker, the shoulders wider, the hips narrower, thighs thicker, arms thicker, and so on.

When you draw the mannequin, still start off with a stick figure first, then add the bulk of the mannequin. Again, remember the butt extends a bit below the triangle that represents the hips and crotch.

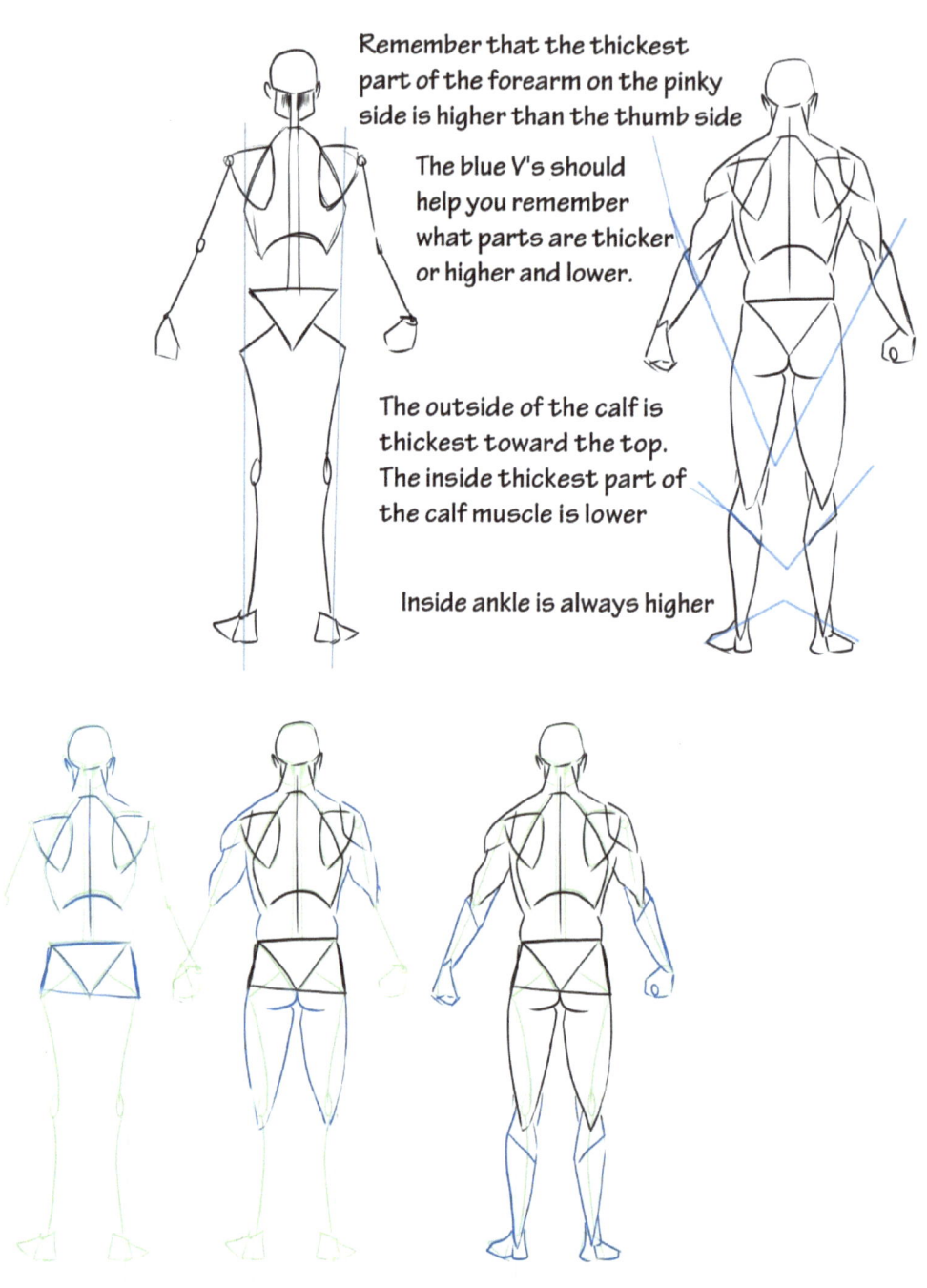

Remember that the thickest part of the forearm on the pinky side is higher than the thumb side

The blue V's should help you remember what parts are thicker or higher and lower.

The outside of the calf is thickest toward the top. The inside thickest part of the calf muscle is lower

Inside ankle is always higher

Side View

The side view of both the skeleton and the mannequin differ a bit, so it might take filling up pages of each to dedicate the new ideas to memory. However, it shouldn't be too difficult.

The measurements remain the same. First, here is a picture of the side view skeleton.

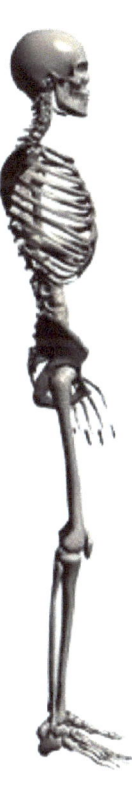

We're going to draw all stick-figure skeleton with a bit more style than the stiff skeleton above.

The placement of the collar bones, ribcage, hips, etc remain the same.

The most important part to remember is how the spine curves from the side view, and how it connects from the back of the skull to the hips.

Learning the side-view of the stick figure is a bit easier because there aren't any differences between the male and female.

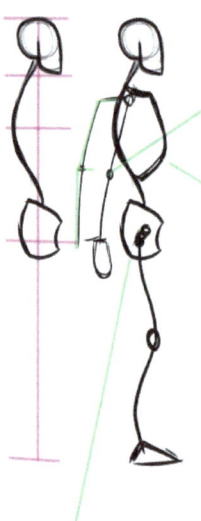

The halfway mark between wrist and shoulder marks the elbow and bottom of ribcage.

Commit to memory the different shape of the ribcage from the sideview

The heal of the foot goes behind the ankle. Draw the foot as a triangle, and be sure the backside of it is on the otherside of the leg.

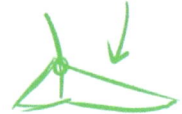

Because the hips look different from the side view we will represent it with a different shape.

Notice that the ribcage extends in front of the spine.

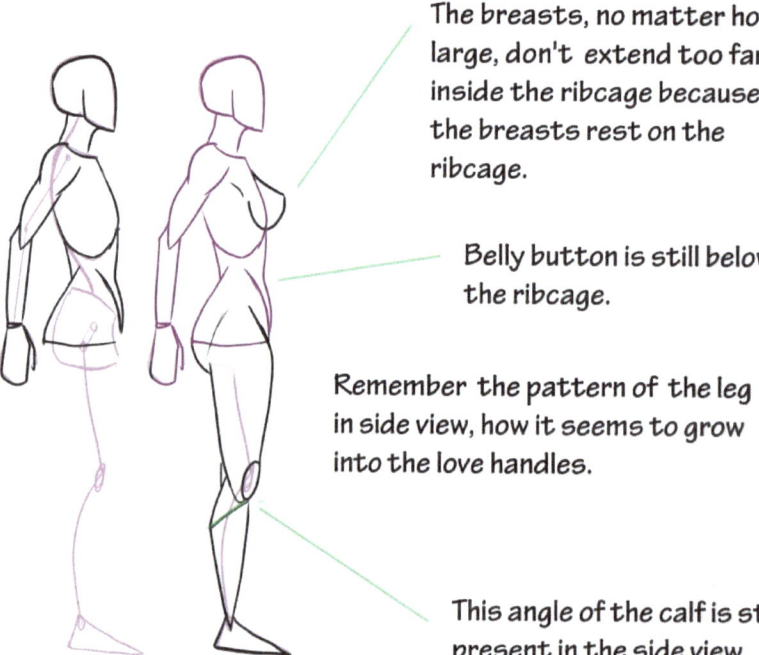

The breasts, no matter how large, don't extend too far inside the ribcage because the breasts rest on the ribcage.

Belly button is still below the ribcage.

Remember the pattern of the leg in side view, how it seems to grow into the love handles.

This angle of the calf is still present in the side view.

The following rhythms will help you remember how the female figure looks from the front view and side view.

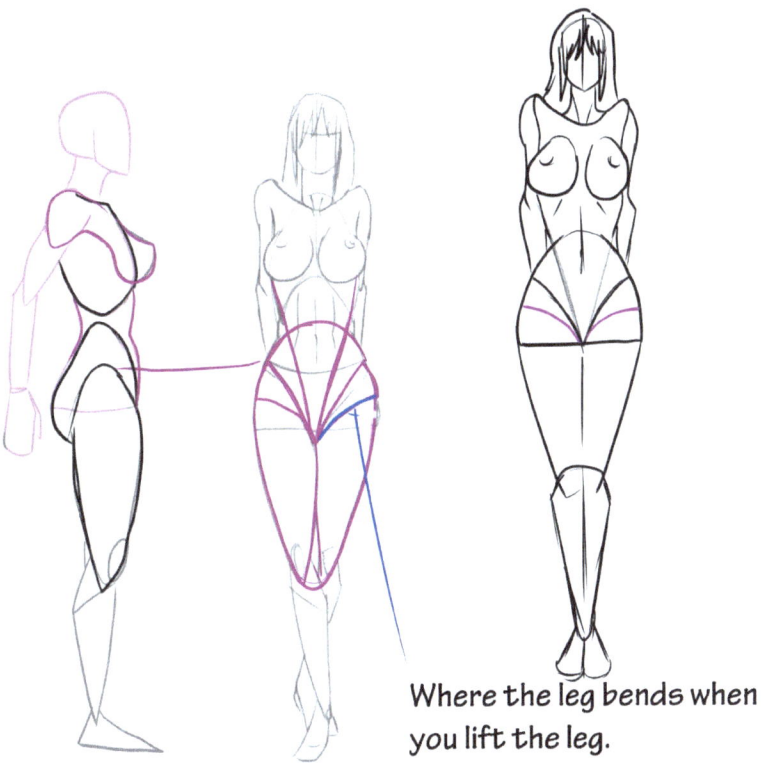

Where the leg bends when you lift the leg.

Now that we know how to draw the figure from the front, side, and back view, we need to learn the most difficult view, the angled view, which is a mix between the side view and the front view. Keep in mind, that in the angled or ¾ view, we are seeing less of the front view, i.e. it is shorter than in front view. Here is an example, using a 3D box.

The horizontal green (or grey) line is the same length.

As you can see, when we turn the box, we see both the side and front view, but less of each. The front and side view get shorter.

The width of the 3/4 view is wider than the front view

These two horizontal lines are the same length

So, when we turn the box in ¾ view, the length is greater because we are seeing both the front and side view, although, both the front and side view are shorter in ¾ view. Let's apply this to the figure.

The shaded planes are the side planes

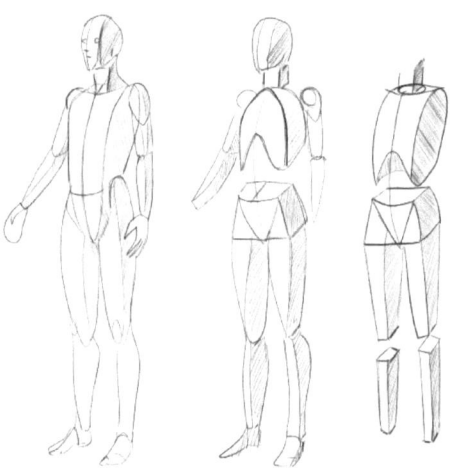

The ¾ view will take you the longest to master, but take the time to practice it by filling up pages of ¾ views, and the hard work will pay off. Before moving on, master the following drawings, of front, side, and ¾ view. This exercise will help you draw the ¾ view.

Here is an easier way to see how side view and front view create the 3/4 view, just like the box.

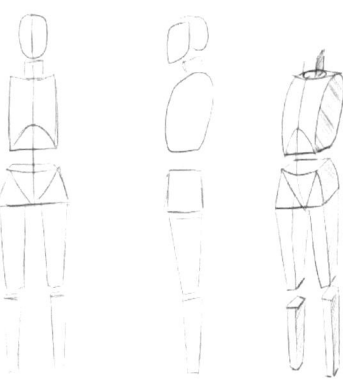

After you have mastered the basic drawings above, so that you can draw the ¾ one from memory, without looking at anything, then try to draw the mannequin in ¾ view.

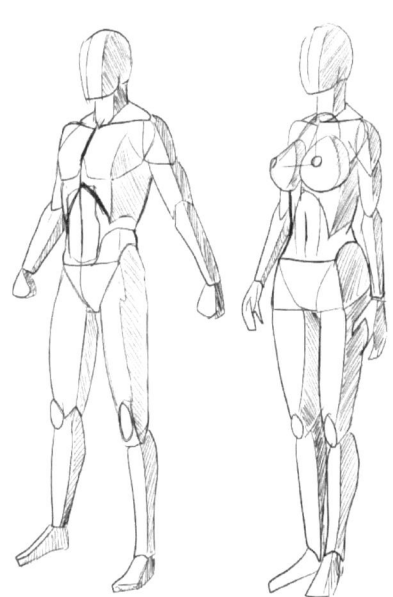

The breasts overlap. We see the one closest to us more round, but the one fartest, we see as if from a side view.

Here is a step by step process you can follow to draw the figure in ¾ view. Mannequin,

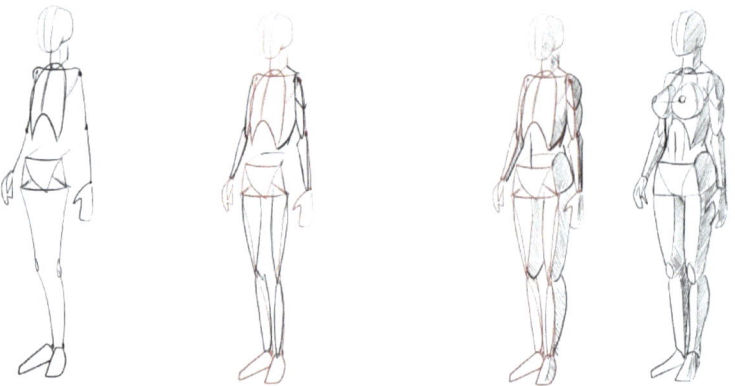

Start with a
skinny skeleton

Add thinner front
view mannequin

Add the side view mannequin

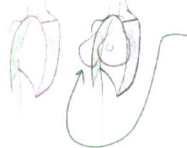 The far breast fits in the farthest portion
of the rib cage, i.e. it doesn't cross the center
line.

Here is an alternative way to draw the ¾ view mannequin. Start with the torso, add a dividing line, then
the limbs.

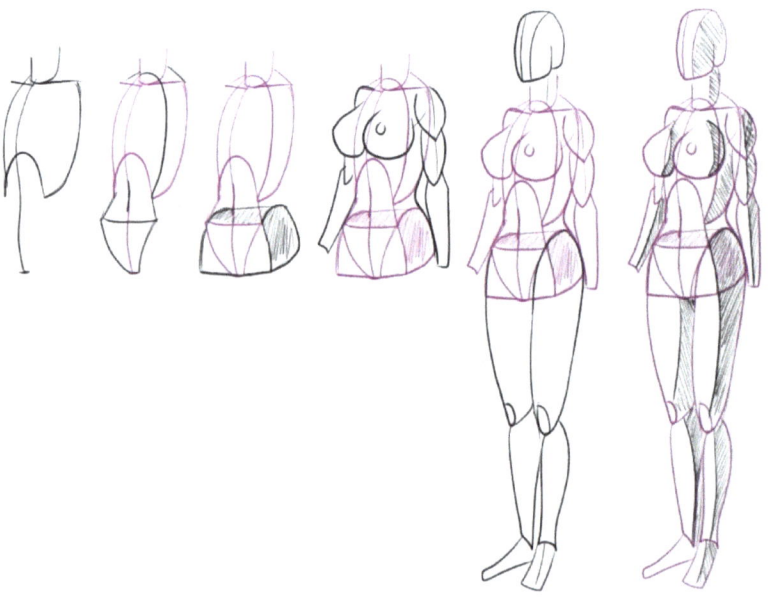

Chapter 3: Muscles and Bones

Now it's time to get to our favorite part, anatomy. Okay, so, I admit, this is the hardest to master, and not the most fun to learn, but your figures will look awesome for learning it.

Anatomy just isn't about muscles and where they attach, but it is also about skin and fat, when it comes to drawing, and of course some bones.

This isn't an anatomy for drawing book, so we will keep it simple and brief, as this topic is huge, and can easily fill up a large book.

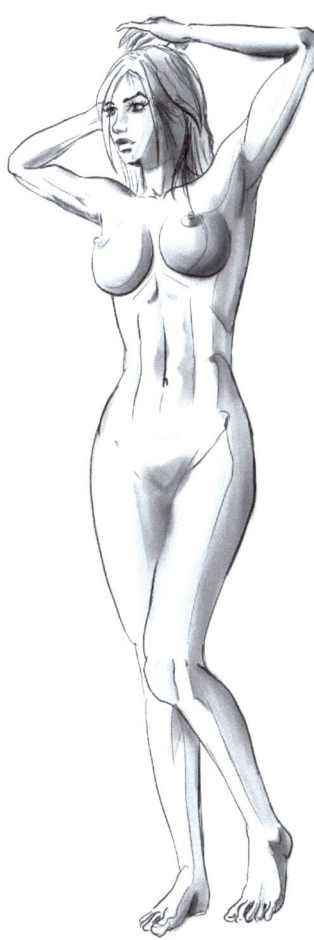

We're going to only go over the outer, visible muscles and some important bones. First, we will start with basic views, front, side, back, and ¾ view, so to better get a 3D understanding of the muscles, which will give us a good 3D understanding of the figure.

This understanding of where muscles attach, will help you draw the figure from imagination, and to invent poses you never saw before. How, you may ask? When you understand where the muscles attach, and their basic movements, then you will be able to logically figure out how a muscle will look when an arm is raised, for example.

I will demonstrate that soon, but first, let's get down the basic views. You really want to master the muscles. Don't just skip over this part. I know how tempting it is, but if you want to draw comics, or concept art, or draw for a living, this is something you need to learn. You must find the drive to read and draw, and draw some more, until you can draw these muscles from these basic views.

Okay, let's get started. Sharpen that pencil.

Important Bones

Some bones, especially on thin people, show through so we can see them, such as the collar bones. Other times, just parts of bones show through the figure. We will now briefly go over the important bones and the parts that show through.

The parts of the bones that can show through, depending on the person, are colored in red, or grey if you are viewing this book in black and white.

I am excluding the parts of the skull, hands, and feet that show through at this point, as this course is focused on the figure.

Focusing on the figure, those bones that show through, are the clavicle (collar bones), sternum, part of the scapular that tops the humerus, the top outer edge of the humerus, the elbow part of the ulna, the wrist part of the ulna, the wrist part of the radius, the patalla (kneecap), part of the tibia, known as the shin, the ankle part of the tibia and fibula.

Here is an image.

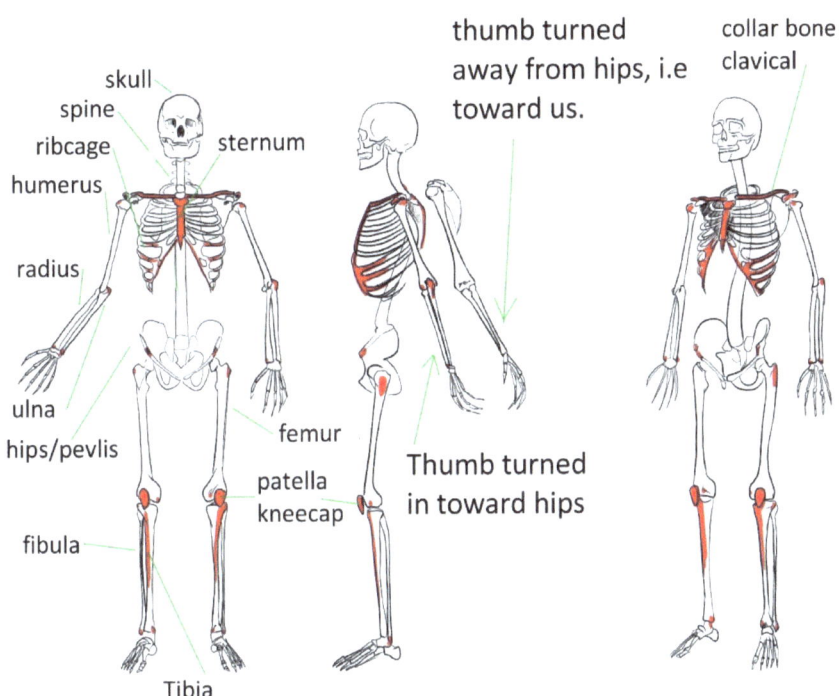

Some quick notes on the bones we see above. Commit to memory that the radius is the large forearm bone that connects to the thumb. Contrary to it is the ulna, which is thinner, and connects to the pinky. So the radius is on the thumb side of the forearm, and the ulna is on the pinky side of the forearm. Believe it or not, knowing this will improve your figure drawings.

Also, the radius is the bone in the forearm that crosses over the ulna when you turn your thumb down. We will get into more details on this in a moment because it's important. It's important because it helps understand why and how the brachioradialis changes shape. This is a muscle we will cover shortly.

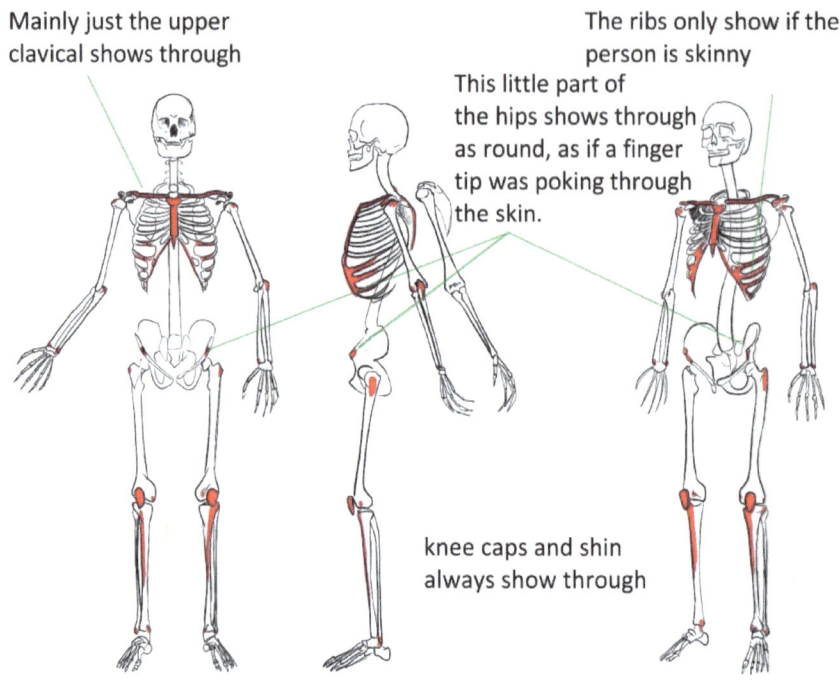

Mainly just the upper clavical shows through

The ribs only show if the person is skinny

This little part of the hips shows through as round, as if a finger tip was poking through the skin.

knee caps and shin always show through

There is no need to memorize the skeleton in great detail. Just memorizing the basic stick-skeleton we covered earlier is enough. However, there are some bones that are important to memorize and understand how they work. First of these is the forearm bones, the radius and ulna.

When the skeleton is facing forward and the palm out, as the skeleton above us on the left, the radius doesn't overlap the ulna.

Here are several views of the arm bones with notes. These aspects of the arm bones are important to memorize for how they move determines how the arm looks because of where the muscles attach, and thus stretch and move. It will make more since when we attach the muscles to the skeleton.

First, we are going to look at the front view of the arm. The lower arm, the forearm bones, ulna and radius, will remain in the position of the palm facing forward, which means the radius is not twisting over the ulna.

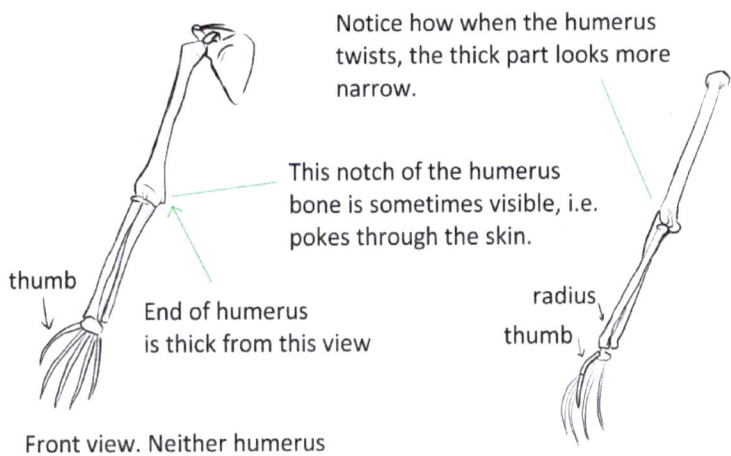

Notice how when the humerus twists, the thick part looks more narrow.

This notch of the humerus bone is sometimes visible, i.e. pokes through the skin.

thumb

End of humerus is thick from this view

radius

thumb

Front view. Neither humerus or forearms bones are twisted.

Palm is facing out.

The thumb is facing us now, but only the humerus is twisted.

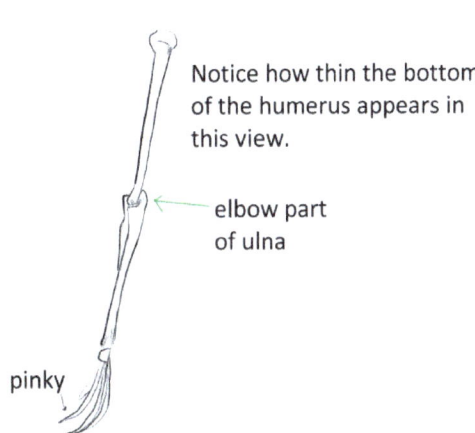

Notice how thin the bottom of the humerus appears in this view.

elbow part of ulna

pinky

This is still the front view of the arm. Now the humerus is twisted so to make the pinky face us. Notice how this reveals the elbow, so that the elbow pokes out.

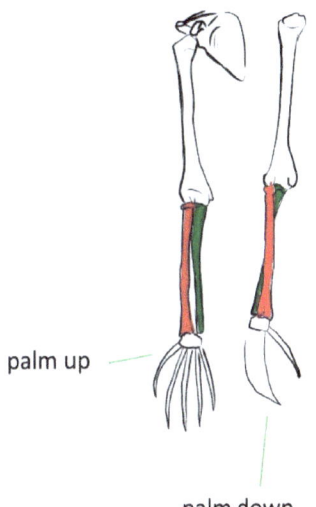

palm up

palm down

When you twist your forearm, so to turn your palm down, or away from us, the radius (red), overlaps the ulna.

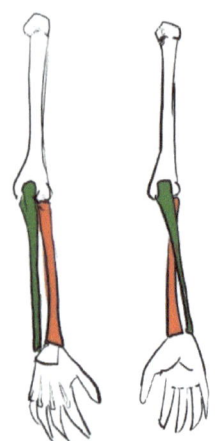

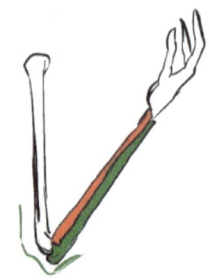

Notice the 90 degree angle and how the elbow is on the forearm, not upper arm.

From the side view, we can see how the unla forms the elbow.

When viewed from the back, the radius appears to go behind the ulna. Remeber the radius always attaches to the thumb side of the hand, and the ulna to the pinky side of the hand.

Notice the boxy shape the albow forms when the arm is bent all the way up.

I highly recommend to draw these skeletal arms several times, so to commit to memory how the radius and ulna works. Also, keep in mind that the humerus is thick at the bottom when viewed from the front or back views, but thin when viewed from the side. One each side of the thick part of the humerus you have bumps that can poke out of the flesh, and thus be visible.

We will go into more details on some bones later. For now let's dive into the main muscles and where they attach. After this, we will get into more details of how they move, flex, and how the body can move.

Muscles

The following information is for the muscles below. We will not go into this much detail for every muscle—just the important muscles. Understanding where some muscles attach is vital to understanding how the muscle moves and changes when the body moves. This way, you can logically figure out how the muscle should stretch.

For example, the peck attaches to the side of the sternum, to part of the collar bone, to part of the ribs, then stretches over and connects to the side of the humerus, toward the top of the humerus. The drawing below will help you see this.

The biceps connect to the two points of the scapula and then to the upper part of the radius, which remember, the radius is on the thumb side of the forearm. Now it makes sense why I had you learn how those bones move. This way, you can figure out how the biceps will stretch when you have your palm facing down, thus causing the radius to roll over the ulna.

This naturally stretches the biceps because when you turn your palm face down, the radius rolls over the ulna, moving, and because the bottom of the biceps is attached to the radius, it stretches, thus the biceps are elongated when the palm is face down.

The deltoid attaches to the other part of the collar bone that the peck doesn't attach to, and works it's way around attaching to the spine of the scapula. I will draw other views of the deltoid in a bit, but for now, here are the muscles discussed so far.

The right humerus is turned
so to make the palm face down,
thus revealing the side of the
humerus.

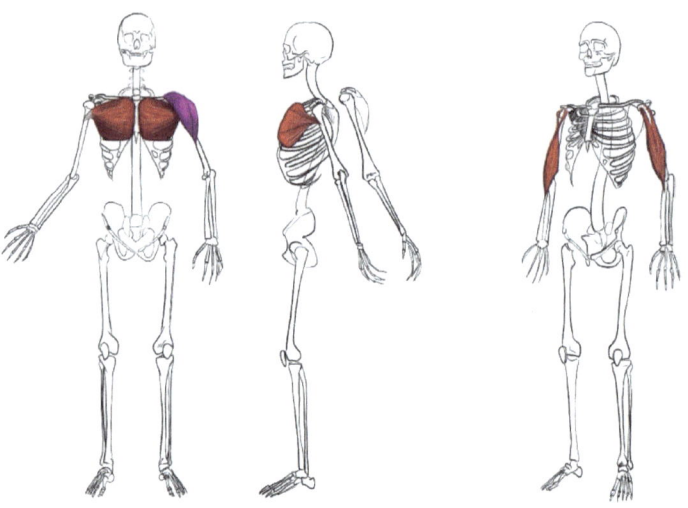

In order, the peck covers the biceps, and the deltoid covers the peck and biceps.

The right humerus is turned
so to make the palm face down,
thus revealing the side of the
humerus.

The deltoid from
top view.

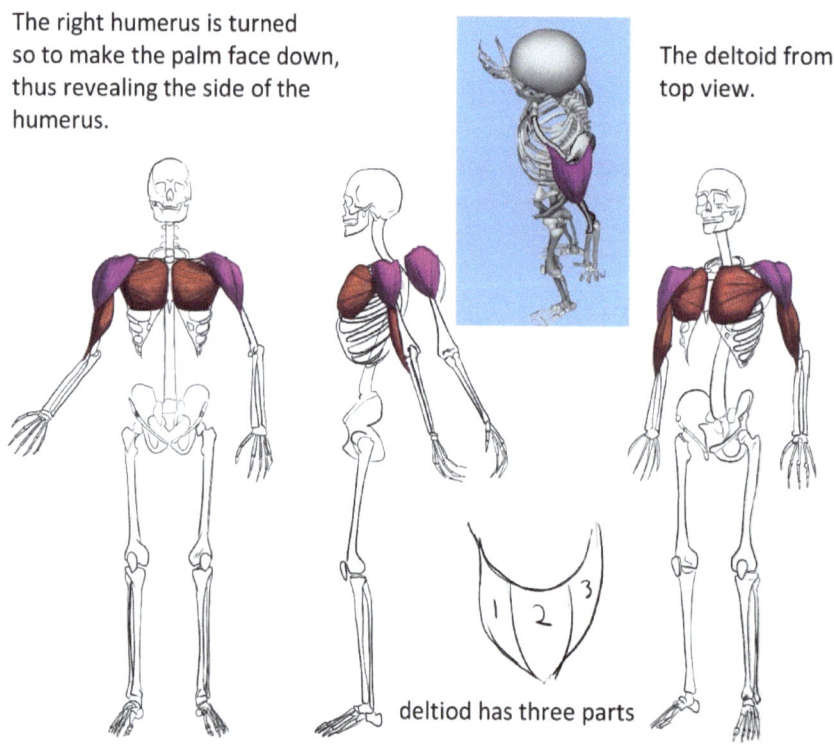

deltiod has three parts

The first part of the deltoid, labeled 1, attaches to the collar bone and is seen from the front. 2 is viewed from the side and attaches to the side of the humerus. 3 is viewed from the back and attaches to the spine of the scapula.

There are a few more muscles I would like to cover where they attach before showing all the outer muscles, then a basic muscle map you can memorize to flesh out your characters.

Two muscles that can seem to drastically change shape are the brachioradialis and the extensor carpi radialis longus. Both are forearm muscles. I think these two muscles give the most confusion to the forearm and how to draw the muscles if palm is up or down. Also, how they stretch and change when the arm is flexed.

Just think of where the muscles are attached and how they logically must stretch when the palm turns face down.

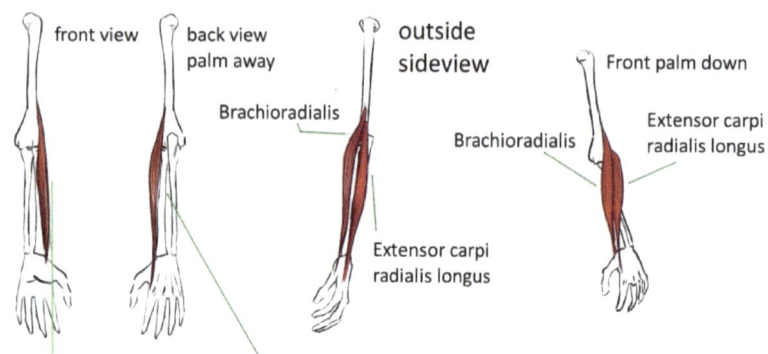

front view

back view
palm away

outside
sideview

Front palm down

Brachioradialis

Brachioradialis

Extensor carpi
radialis longus

Extensor carpi
radialis longus

Brachioradialis attaches to
the lower humerus and to
the metacarporal bones just
above the thumb. Think of it
as attaching to the thumb.

Extensor Carpi Radialis Longus
connects to a slightly lower part
of the humerus than Brachioradialis.
It then connects to the top part of the
index finger.

When the palm is face down, so that the radius
overlaps the ulna, then the brachioradialis must
stretch around the arm. Just think of where it is
connected. Look at the front view, on the far left
of this image. That is palm up. When the hand
turns over, palm down, then the brachioradialis
must turn over with it because it is attached to
the thumb. Because the Extensor Carpi Radialis
Longus is attached to the index finger, it follows
the brachioradilis. Think of these two muscles as
kind of connecting together. They go with each
other when the arm moves.

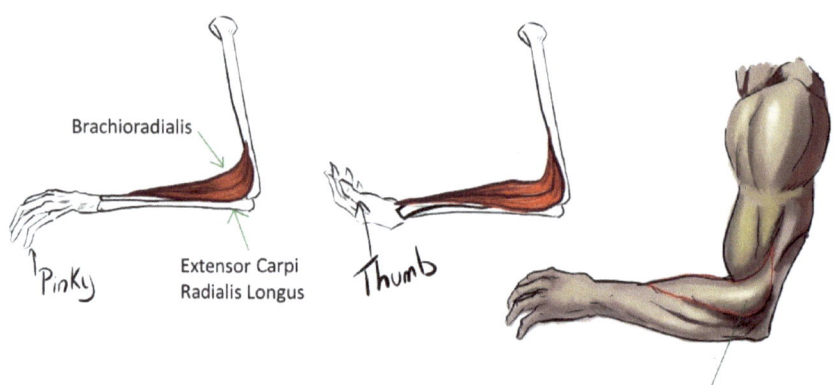

Brachioradialis

Extensor Carpi
Radialis Longus

Pinky

Thumb

These two muscles form the bulge outline in red.
Think about the elbow as a flat plane.

Notice how when the palm is turned face up, we see more of the
brachioradialis. This is because it is connected to the thumb
side of the forearm. When the palm is face down, the thumb
turns away from us, and thus we see less of the brachioradialis.

If you know how the bones move, and where these two
muscles attach, then you can figure out how they will
twist and stretch.

Continuing with the muscles of the figure, which are important to learn, we will now learn how to draw the torso muscles.

Rectus Abdominis (abs) – The abs connect from the costal cartilages of ribs 4 to 7 all the way down to the pelvis.

External Oblique – Sometimes partly called love handles. It is most visible from the side of the body, but in most humans it is not very visible because it is covered with fat. It attaches to upper ribs and all the way down to the iliac crest of the pelvis.

Serratus Anterior – It is most visible from the side of the body. It connects to the 1st to 8th ribs and to the scapula. This muscle is what causes the lines on the side of the ribcage, often seen in super heroes.

Latissimus Dorsi – Also called lats. It connects to the upper, backside of the humerus, and along the lower part of the spin, and then connects to the back part of the pelvis. It is mostly visible from the back.

Abs = red
Oblique = yellow
Serratus = green
lats = blue

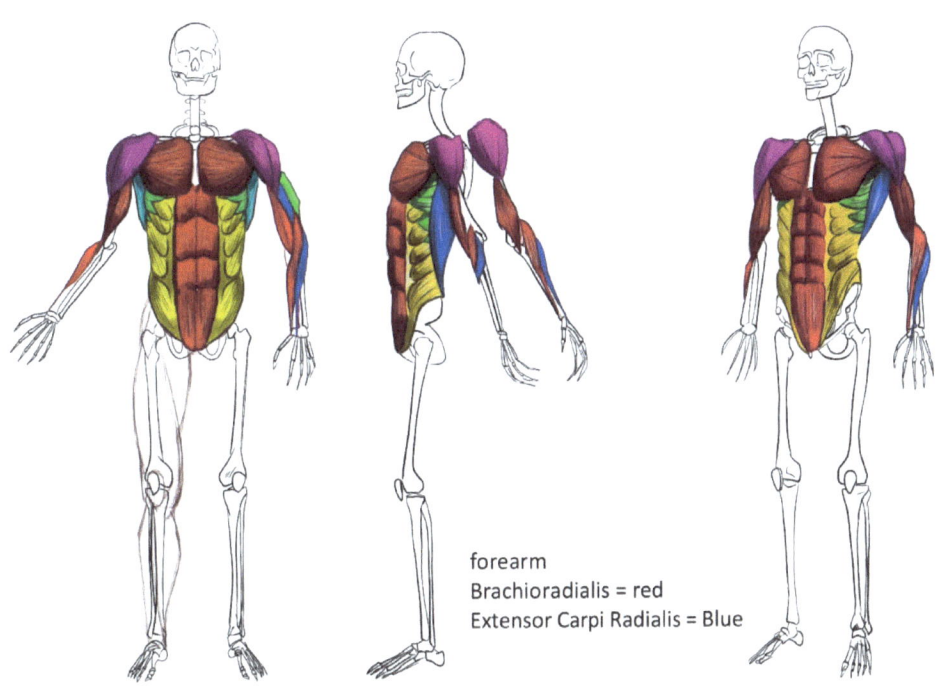

forearm
Brachioradialis = red
Extensor Carpi Radialis = Blue

The muscles we covered so far are easy to learn. However, the forearm muscles can be really tricky to learn because of how they move. So before we continue to learn the rest of the muscles, let's focus on the rest of the forearm muscles.

Think of the palm side of the forearm as having three major muscles that can be grouped together, the knuckle side to have four major muscles that can be grouped together, and finally two side muscles for the thumb side, and one for the pinky side. If you group the forearm together like this, it makes it much easier to memorize and draw.

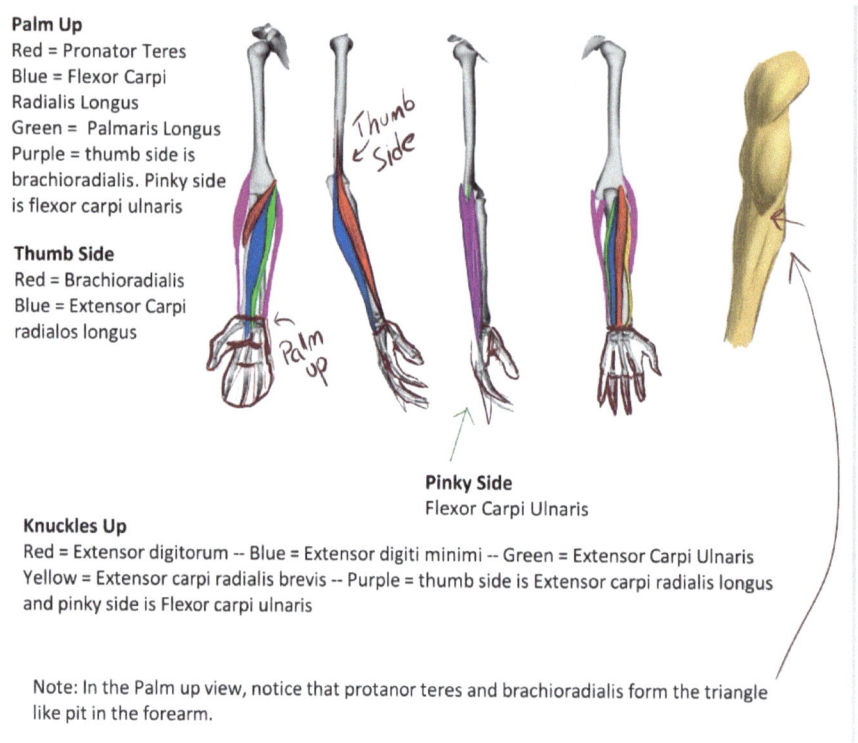

Palm Up
Red = Pronator Teres
Blue = Flexor Carpi Radialis Longus
Green = Palmaris Longus
Purple = thumb side is brachioradialis. Pinky side is flexor carpi ulnaris

Thumb Side
Red = Brachioradialis
Blue = Extensor Carpi radialos longus

Pinky Side
Flexor Carpi Ulnaris

Knuckles Up
Red = Extensor digitorum -- Blue = Extensor digiti minimi -- Green = Extensor Carpi Ulnaris
Yellow = Extensor carpi radialis brevis -- Purple = thumb side is Extensor carpi radialis longus and pinky side is Flexor carpi ulnaris

Note: In the Palm up view, notice that protanor teres and brachioradialis form the triangle like pit in the forearm.

In this next drawing, I include all the forearm muscles. It can be challenging to imagine what muscles you will see when the arm is viewed at different angles and the pam is either up or down, i.e. the forearm is either twisted or not. However, if you think about where those muscles attach, then you can figure out what muscles you should see.

Just remember the picture above. There are three outer muscles you see on the underside of the forearm, and four major muscles you see on the top side of the forearm. Then, on the thumb side, you see two major muscles, the brachioradialis and the extensor carpi radialis longus. On the pinky side you see one muscles that splits as if it is two muscles, the flexor carpi ulnaris.

Also, in the next drawing, we are going to introduce four new visible muscles of the upper arm...

Biceps—We covered already.

Brachialis—From the outer side view, it is between the biceps and triceps.

Triceps—Are mostly seen from side views or back views, however, you can see a little of the triceps even from some front views, as it is larger than the biceps.

Coracobrachialis—Is viewed on the inside view, and is seen between the biceps and triceps.

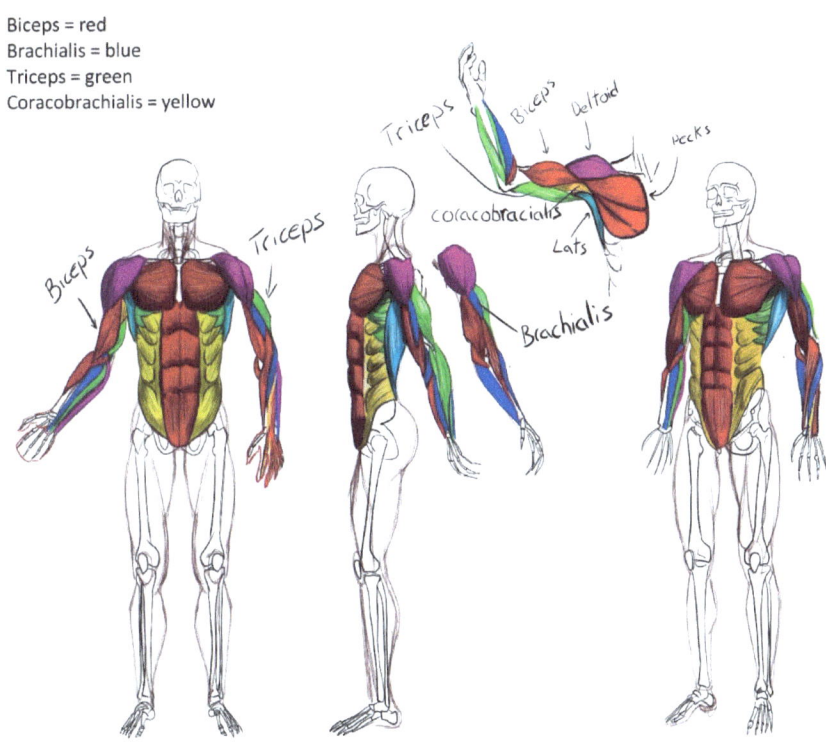

Next we will add the visible leg muscles. I know it can be boring to learn muscles, but learning them is very important. First we will go over the upper leg muscles. You don't need to memorize all the names, nor do you need to memorize all the muscles here, but they will give you a better understanding of the muscle map that we will go over later, the muscle map that will include skin.

I use the same colors for the same muscles, so you can tell when that same muscle is viewed from a different angle. However, because colors are limited, I have used some colors more than once for different muscles.

There are four muscles in the front leg you should be concerned with. The gracilis, vastus medialis, vastus lateralis, and sartorius.

Upper Leg Muscles front view
red = rectus femoris -- blue = vastus medialis -- green = vastus lateralis -- yellow = sartorius
violet (outside leg) = tensor fasciae latae -- grey violet (inside leg by crotch) = gracilis -- pink-purple
(next to gracilis = adductor longus -- teal = pectineus -- red (next to pectineus) = iliacus

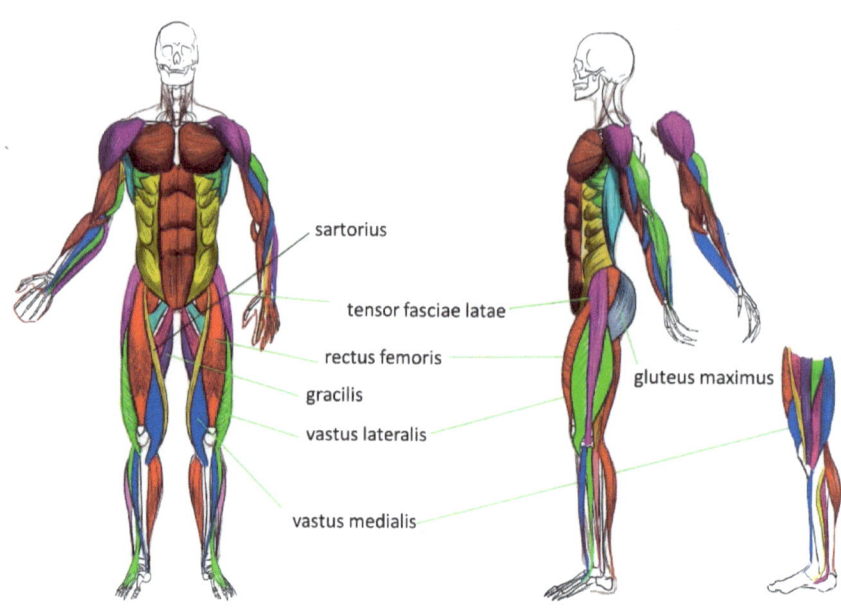

I drew all the outer muscles, but they aren't all necessary to learn. I'm only showing them, so you can relate the muscles to the muscle map with skin on it, which we will do next. However, seeing all the muscles without skin and fat really helps to understand why the surface muscles look the way they do.

From the back view there are only a few muscles to be concerned with, the calves, biceps femoris, semitendinosus, vastus lateralis, and semimembranosus. The biceps femoris and semitendinosus, you can think of as one muscle.

The outside, big toe side of the lower leg, you only need to remember the calves, tibialis anterior, soleus, and flexor digitorum longus. The last two, you can think of as one muscle, as that is how it shows up in defined people.

The inside, pinky toe side of the lower leg, you only need to memorize the calves and tibialis anterior.

The tibialis anterior is basically your skin muscle.

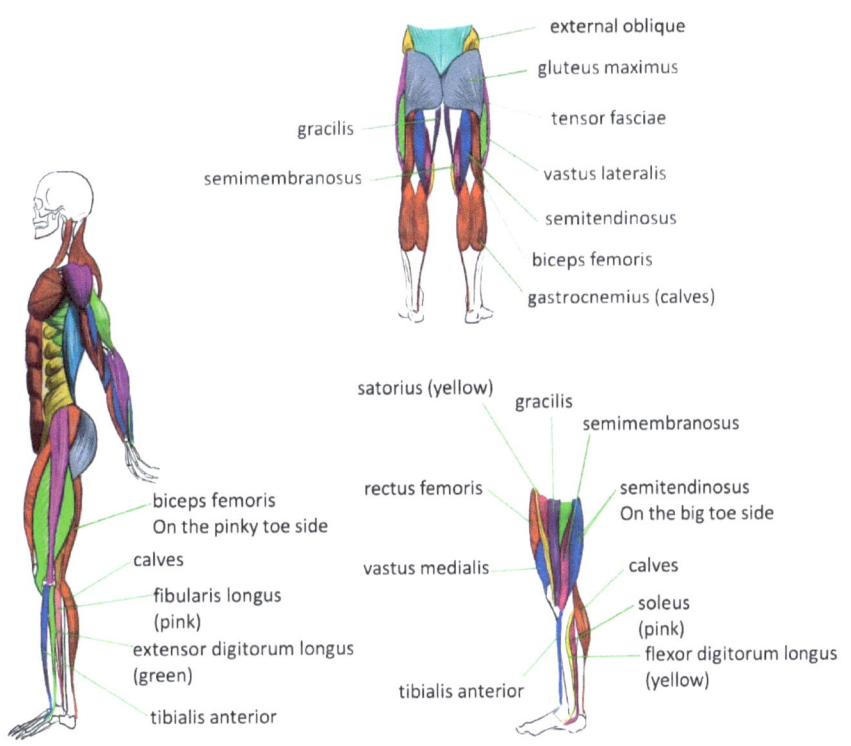

external oblique

gluteus maximus

tensor fasciae

gracilis

vastus lateralis

semimembranosus

semitendinosus

biceps femoris

gastrocnemius (calves)

satorius (yellow)

gracilis

semimembranosus

rectus femoris

semitendinosus
On the big toe side

biceps femoris
On the pinky toe side

calves

calves

fibularis longus
(pink)

soleus
(pink)

vastus medialis

flexor digitorum longus
(yellow)

extensor digitorum longus
(green)

tibialis anterior

tibialis anterior

The last muscles we will cover are the neck muscles and upper back muscles. We will go a bit more into muscles after we learn and memorize to draw the basic muscle map onto our mannequins.

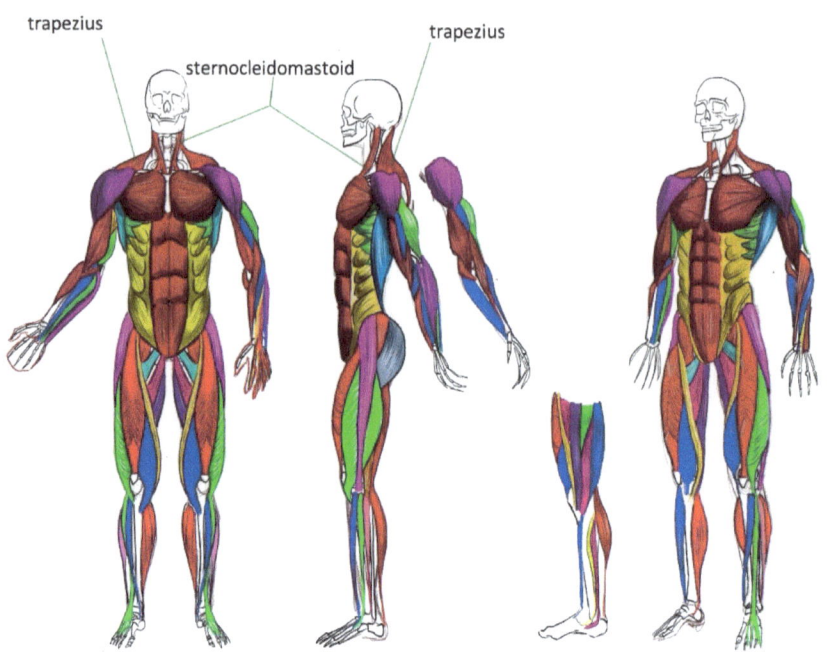

These neck muscles are probably the easiest to grasp, but the whole next area after we add skin can be difficult to draw correctly from imagination, but if you first learn these important muscles, drawing the neck will be much easier.

The traps are a back muscle, which wrap around and partly connect to the collar bone. You can then see a gap between the traps and the sterno, short for sternocleidomastoid. Understanding this gap is crucial to drawing the neck correctly.

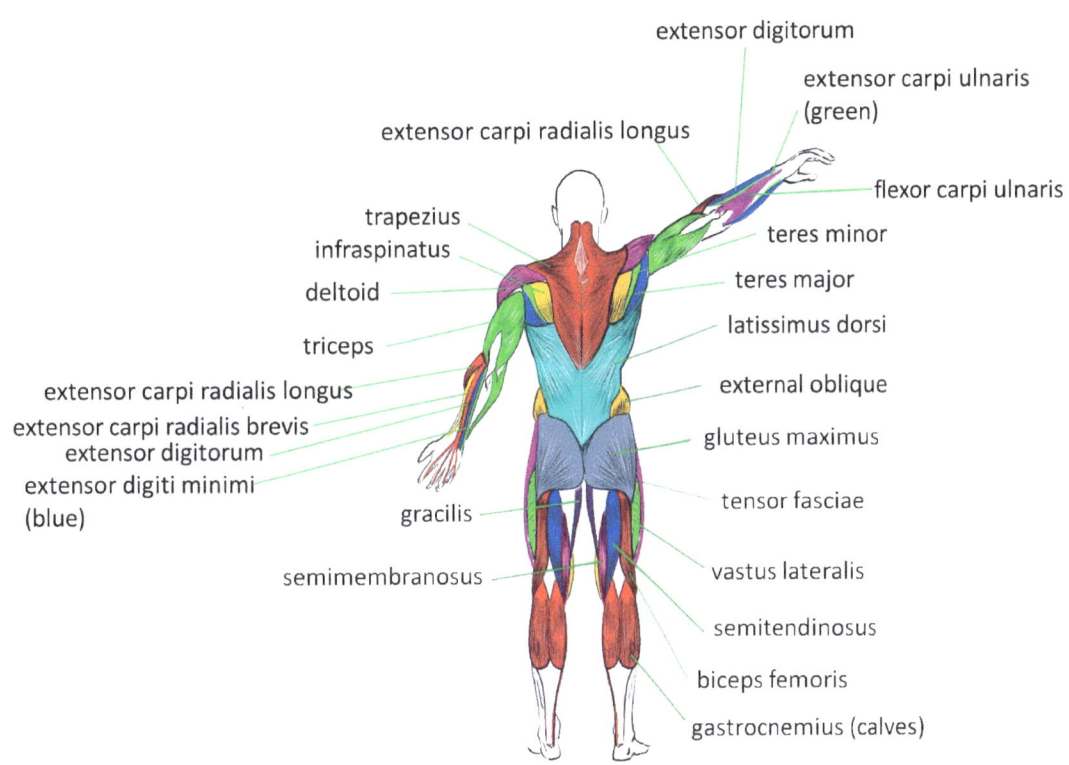

extensor digitorum

extensor carpi ulnaris
(green)

extensor carpi radialis longus

flexor carpi ulnaris

trapezius

teres minor

infraspinatus

teres major

deltoid

latissimus dorsi

triceps

external oblique

extensor carpi radialis longus

gluteus maximus

extensor carpi radialis brevis

extensor digitorum

tensor fasciae

extensor digiti minimi
(blue)

gracilis

vastus lateralis

semimembranosus

semitendinosus

biceps femoris

gastrocnemius (calves)

As you can see, the traps and lats are the two largest muscles that make up the back. Also, you can see when the arm is raised some muscles stretch, like the lats, because the lats partly connect to the humerus bone as does the deltoid and other muscles.

Chapter 4: Muscle Map and Skin

Muscle Map

The muscle map is important to learn, so please take the time to draw the muscle maps several times. First draw one of them a few times from this book, then try drawing it from imagination. Keep going back and forth like that until you can draw it successfully from imagination. After that, move onto the next muscle map.

These muscle maps are how the body looks with skin and fat, although, a very little amount of fat.

Because these are muscle maps, I chose boring poses that best show the most amount of muscle variations you will run into. Carefully, look at these muscle maps, then look at the actual muscles we covered in chapter 3, to see how many muscles combine together as if one muscle.

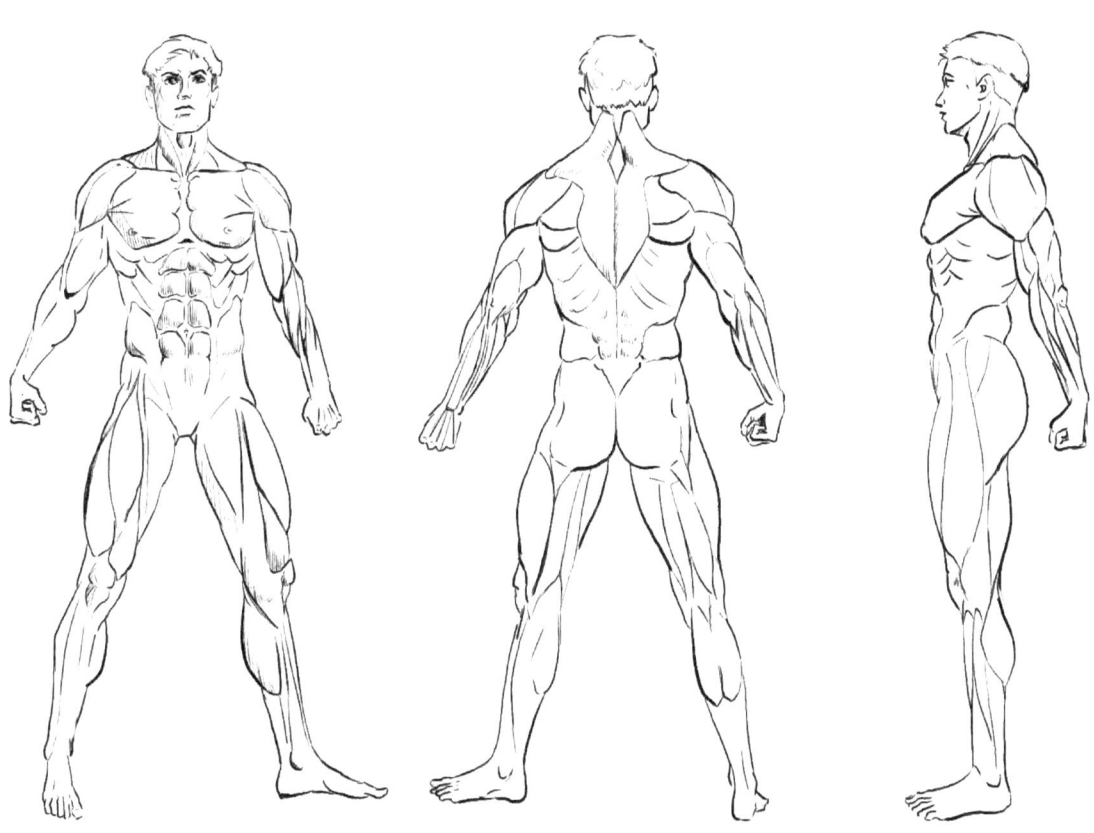

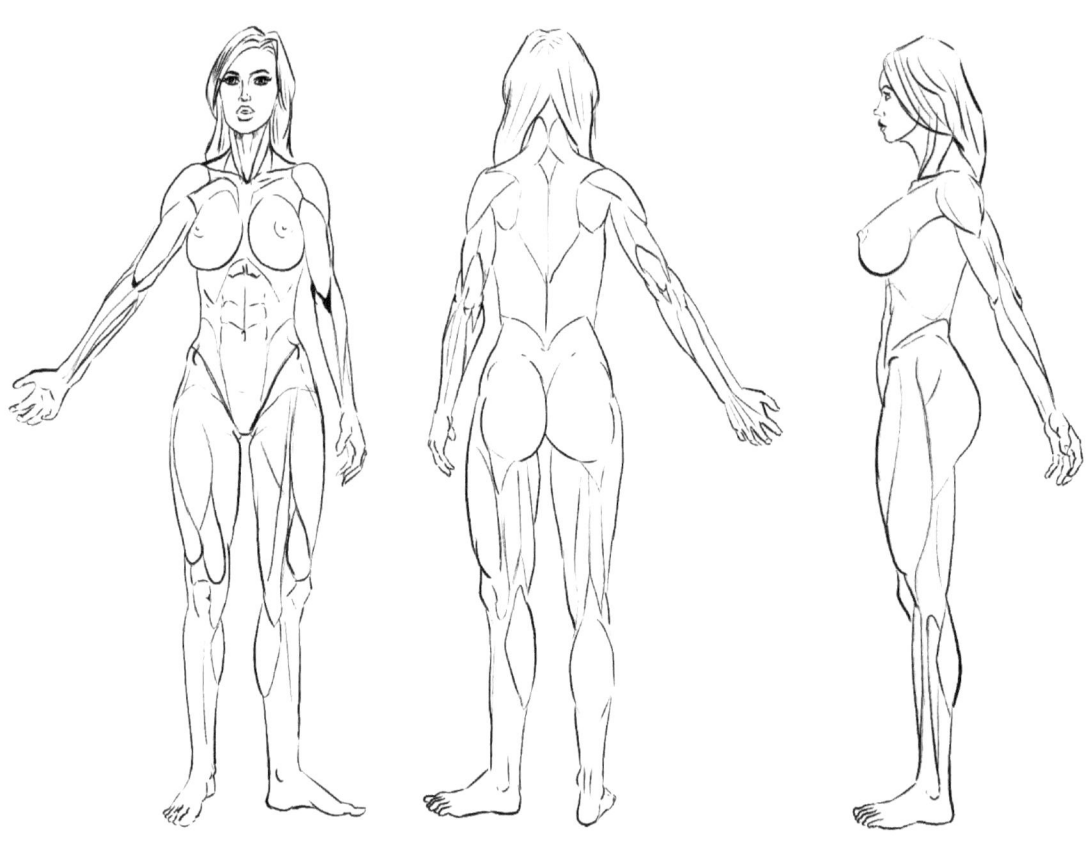

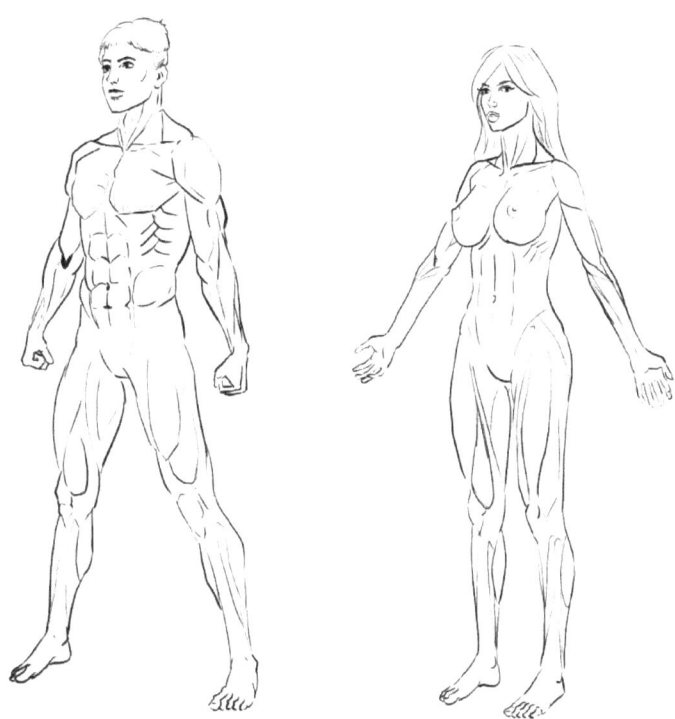

Now we take what we have learned about the muscles, bones, and muscle map, then simplify a bit in order to get a more realistic person. Fat and skin make the muscles less defined. Think of the difference between Bruce Lee and Nicholas Cage. Both are skinny, but we could see most of Bruce Lee's muscles because he had less fat between them. But most people have a higher body fat percent than Bruce Lee had. Right now, we have learned enough to draw people like Bruce Lee, but to draw other body types, we need to learn how figures look with skin and fat on them.

So first we will draw a female with a normal amount of fat on her. She will be thin, but without much definition. This helps to learn where fat builds up between the muscles. Then we will get into where fat builds up.

When drawing the female or male with less definition, think of the body as made of clay, then smooth out the muscles, and add some clay to help smooth the transition. Sculpting the figure out of clay helped me learn the human body more than anything else has.

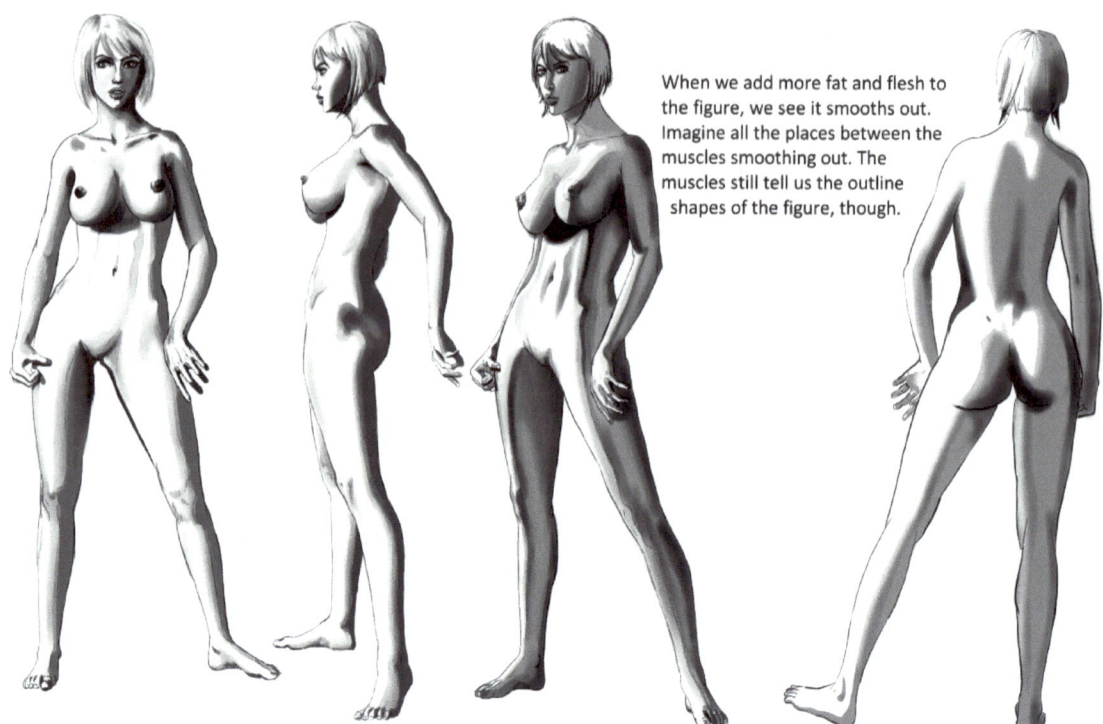

When we add more fat and flesh to the figure, we see it smooths out. Imagine all the places between the muscles smoothing out. The muscles still tell us the outline shapes of the figure, though.

When shading breasts, keep the basic form in mind.

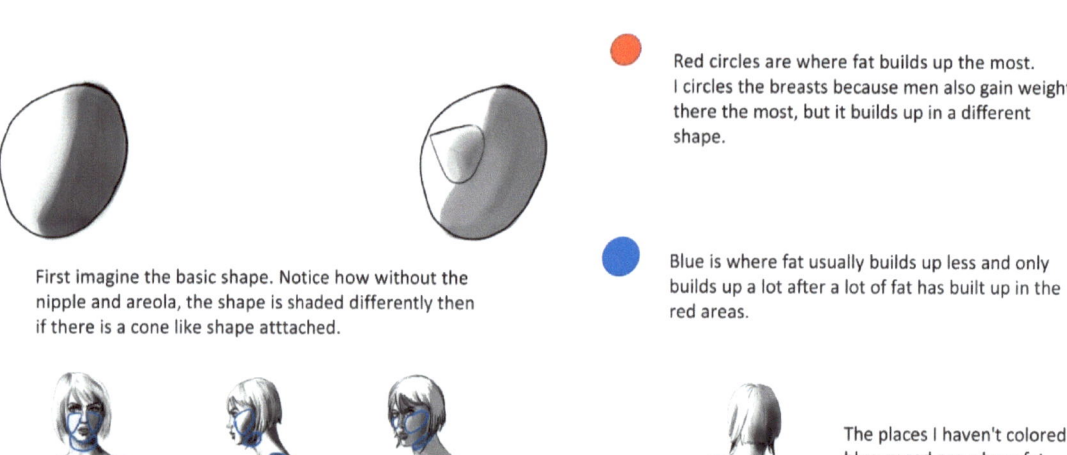

First imagine the basic shape. Notice how without the nipple and areola, the shape is shaded differently then if there is a cone like shape atttached.

Red circles are where fat builds up the most. I circles the breasts because men also gain weight there the most, but it builds up in a different shape.

Blue is where fat usually builds up less and only builds up a lot after a lot of fat has built up in the red areas.

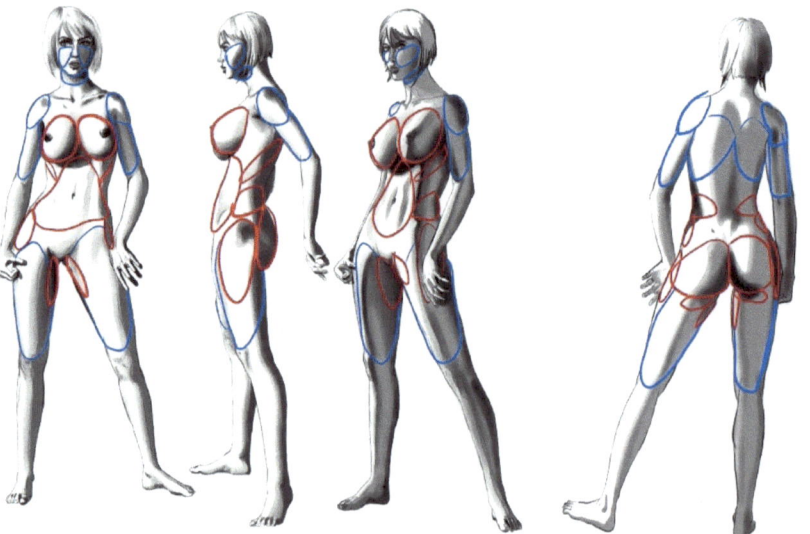

The places I haven't colored blue or red are where fat builds up the least.

Fat can build up in different ways, forming different body types. Typically, though, females develop more fat in the lower region, by hips and butt, and men in the upper body, especially the stomach. In fact, a lot of men can have a good amount of upper body fat, yet a normal butt and normal legs.

When drawing fat on the body, keep gravity in mind. It will pull the fat down, even when the body is in motion. Often when beginning artists draw breasts, for example, they draw them like coconuts, unaffected by gravity. Keep gravity in mind for all body parts.

Here are some basic body types to keep in mind.

Hour glass figure: Mainly gains weight in the breast and hips and butt.

Very skinny. Lack of muscle and fat. Draw with knowledge of skeleton.

Pear shape: Most of the fat develops in the hips, butt, breasts, and a but in the belly.

Apple shape: More of the fat develops on the upper body first. In this case the person has gained a lot of weight.

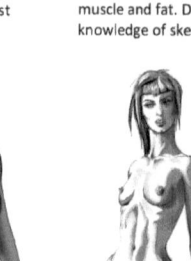
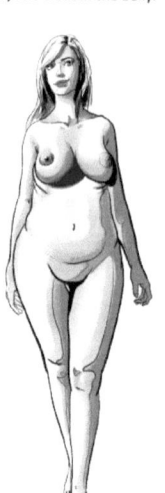
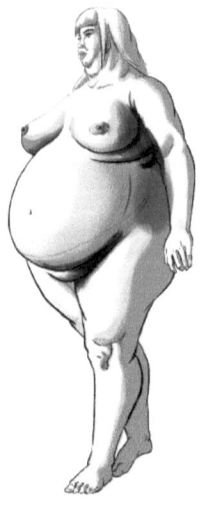

The fat from the pecks, run around the side and to the back of the body. Then you typically have two or three folds of fat below that, the bottom being the love handles.

We can see these same three folds of fat move around to the back. The breast fat moves around to the back, but move up almost along the scapula.

Females will have the same fat build up, even if they are skinnier.

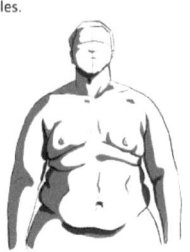
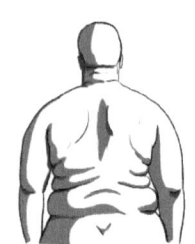
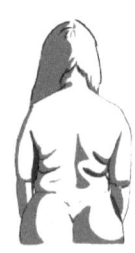

Apple shape: Men typically gain wait up top. They can have a huge beer belly, yet normal butt and thighs.

Skinny: This is the overly skinny body for a male. Rely on bones a lot when you draw such characters.

A skinny yet overweight body type. They mainly gain weginht in their belly.

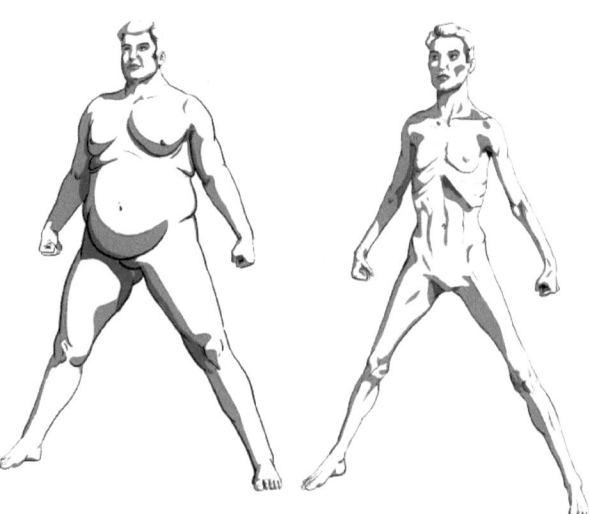
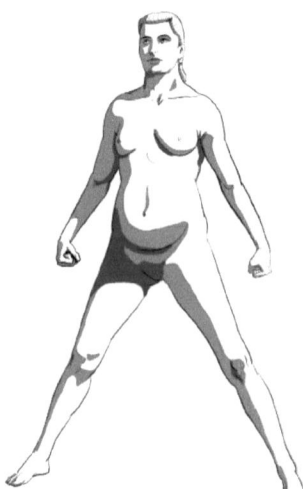

Chapter 5: Body in Motion

Limits of body movement

Before we draw some poses with all the knowledge we have learned, it is important that we learn the limits of the body. Each limb can only move so far, depending on how flexible the person is. However, we need not limit our characters to the limits of the body. We can make the body move in ways a real person could never, and still with logic, make the pose believable.

However, knowing the limits will help you draw the figure.

We learn the extremes of each movement, then we can imagine the movements that happen between them.

The arm in green, notice how when it is lifted high, it lift's the breasts. This is because the pecks are attached to the humorus bone.

Notice this V shape that the pecks form when the arm is down

The black drawing of this arm is pulled back in space

The red lines are the exact same lengths

Keep the basic skeleton in mind when drawing people bent over.

Gravity pulls the breasts down

When the knee bends all the way notice, how the calf pushes into the thigh. Also, notice how when these two muscles and fat press against each other, they form a crease. That muscles, like with the one on the arm, turn into a U shape.

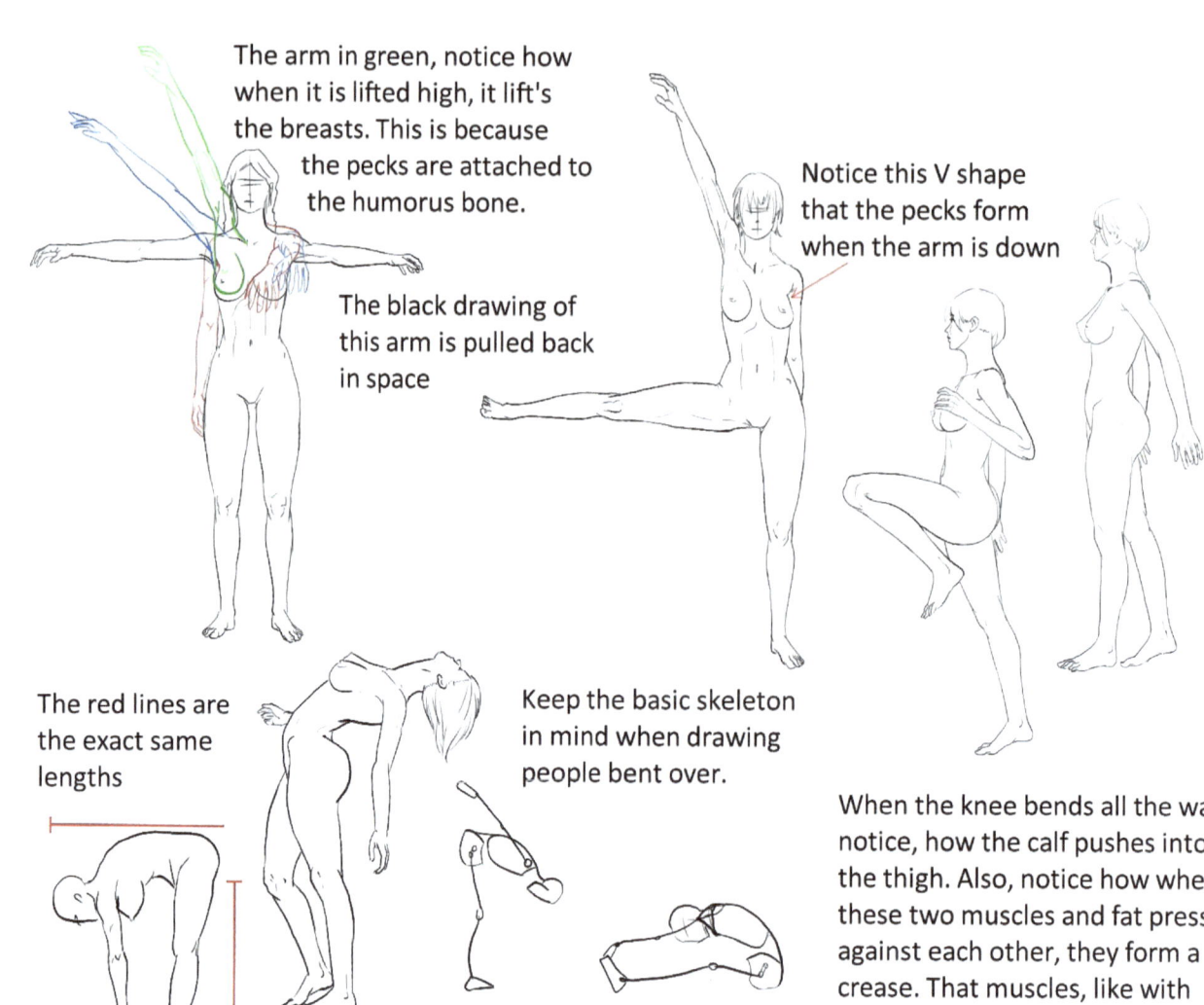

Form of the Body

Before we draw some cool poses, using all the knowledge we have learned, let us learn the 3D form of the body. If we can see the body as a 3D form, it makes drawing poses much easier.

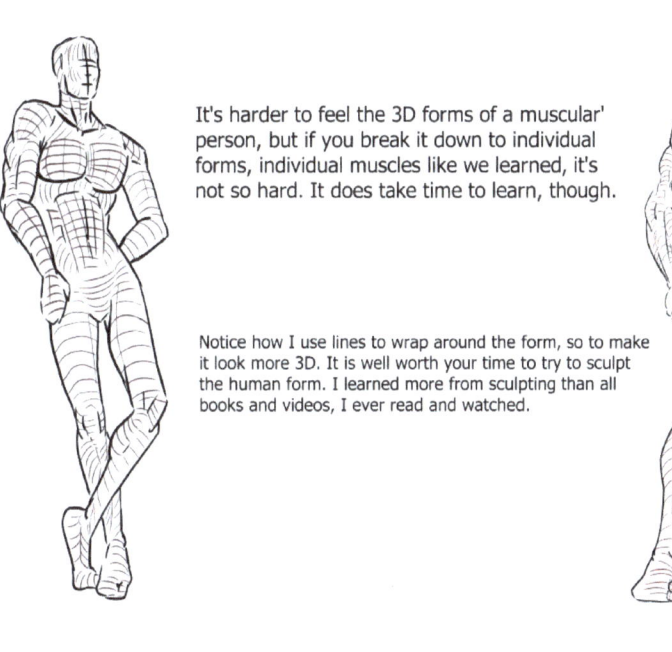

It's harder to feel the 3D forms of a muscular person, but if you break it down to individual forms, individual muscles like we learned, it's not so hard. It does take time to learn, though.

Notice how I use lines to wrap around the form, so to make it look more 3D. It is well worth your time to try to sculpt the human form. I learned more from sculpting than all books and videos, I ever read and watched.

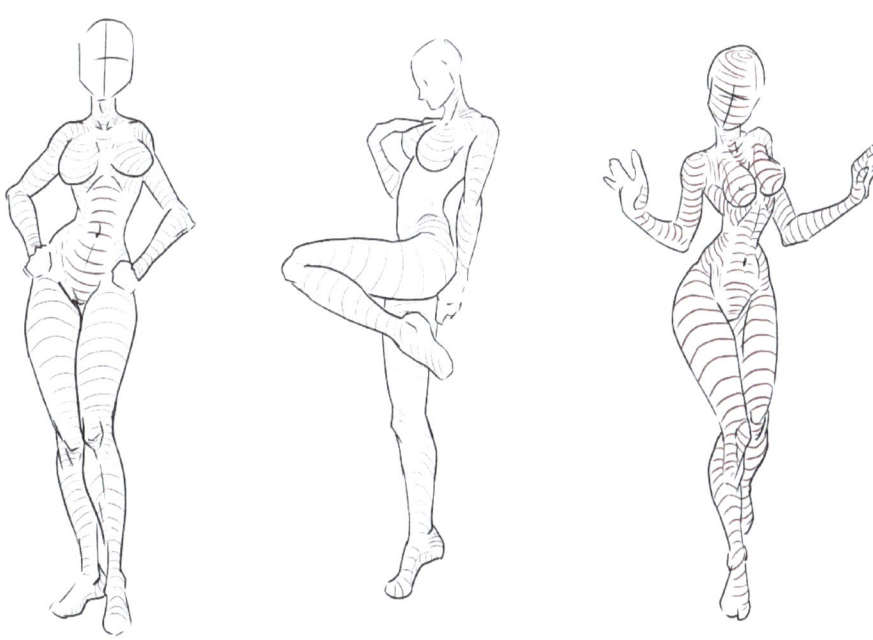

Chapter 6: Drawing humans of different ages

When drawing humans of different ages, the head size changes slightly. I have simplified it so you can get realistic ages without having to memorize much information. For this reason, we only use 3 head sizes, adult, teen, and kid.

Each head is only a tad smaller than the next, but it makes a huge difference in body size and believability of the age. A toddler with an adult size or even teen size head wouldn't look right, although Manga uses this all the time, so for that style it works. Keep style in mind.

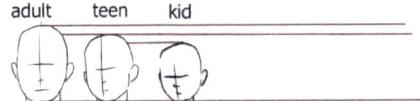

adult   teen   kid

Because kids pretty much look the same, if male or female, I only put teen and adults as different. I also skipped the 8 headed tall adult because we already covered it.

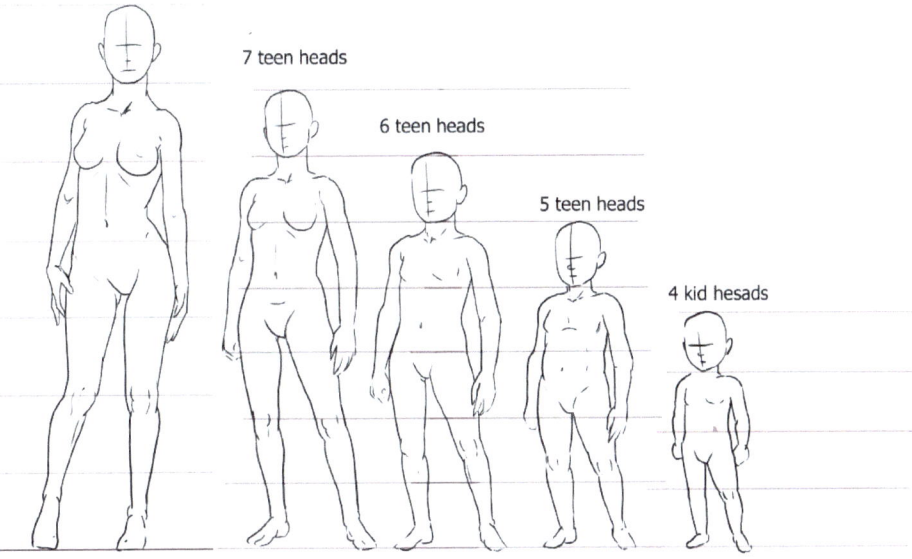

7 adult heads

7 teen heads

6 teen heads

5 teen heads

4 kid hesads

7 adult heads

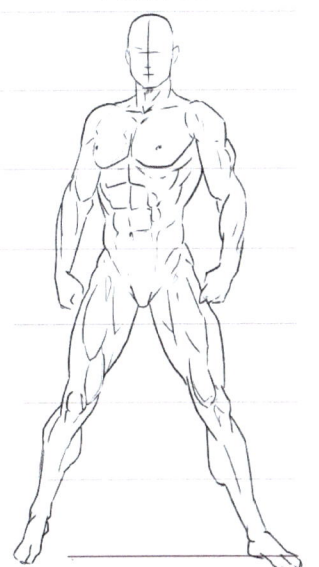

7 teen heads

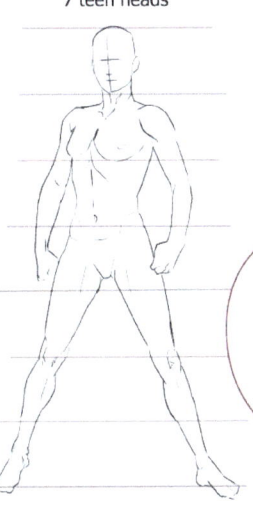

You can draw a 5 headed adult, with an adult size head and make him very buff like Wolverine. So these aren't the only types of bodies to draw. Mix it up.

The same principles apply to always fine the elbows and bottom of rib cage. You draw a line from the top of the shoulder to the bottom of the crotch, then divide that in half. The middle point is the elbow and the bottom of the rib cage.

Also, regardless of the length of legs, you divde from the bottom fo the crotch to the feet in half. The knees fit above that. Sometimes in toddlers, the knees fit on that line.

This is a universal measurement regardless of age or height. You draw a line from the top of the shoulder to the bottom of the crotch. Divide that in half.

That is the elbow and the bottom of the rib cage.

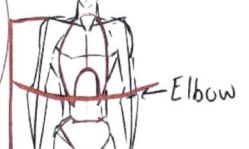

Elbow

Chapter 7: Popular poses: putting it all together

For the final chapter, we will draw several popular poses you might find in fine art, comics, concept art, etc. I have chosen particular poses that you should draw many times, as those poses will help you memorize the parts of the body and angles to draw many other poses. That is, after you have these poses memorized, you will be able to apply the knowledge you have learned in this book and invent new poses without much difficulty.

Do keep in mind that drawing the human figure from imagination is not an easy task, but this book will make it easier for you.

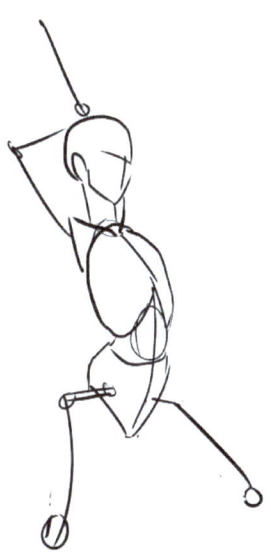

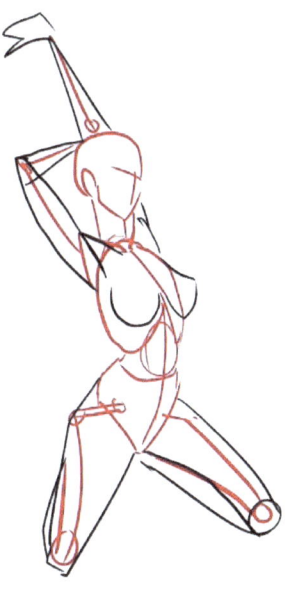

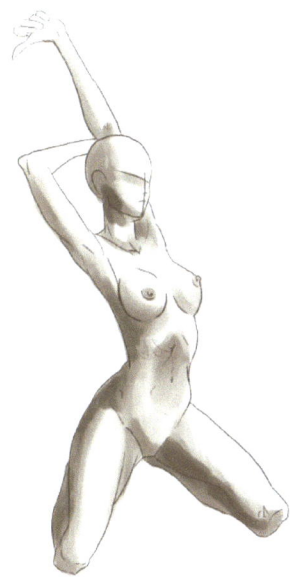

Somtimes it is easier to start with a stick figure, but be sure to add movement and gesture.

Build form on top of either yoiur gesture or stick figure. Use basic shapes.

Lastly add anatomy.

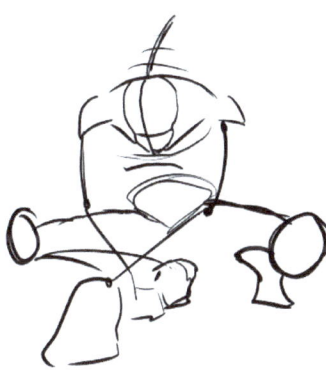

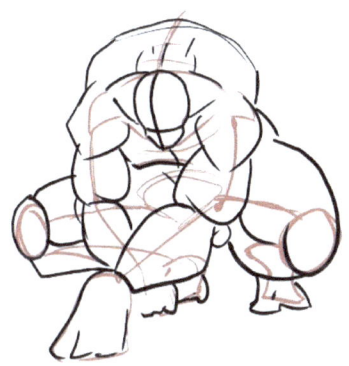

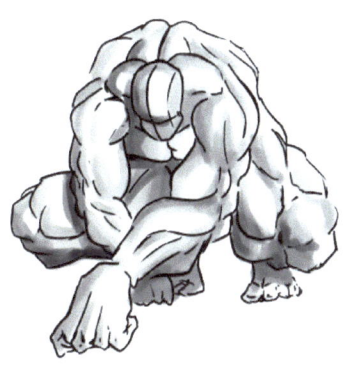

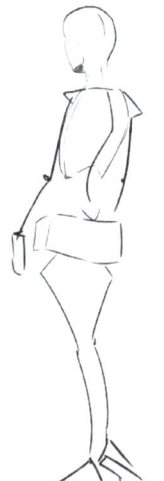

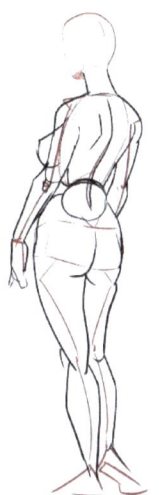

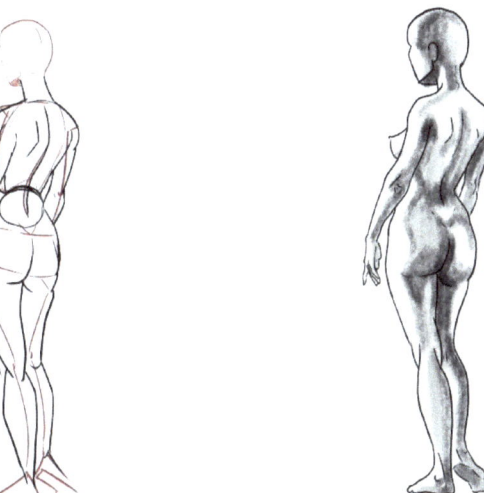

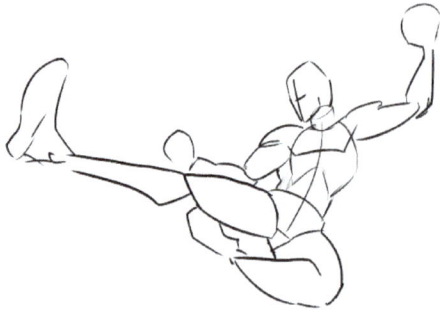 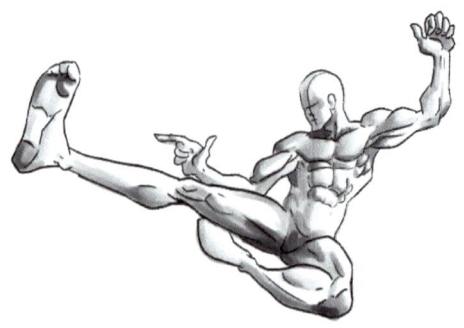

Sometimes, it is easier to start with basic shapes that show movement and gesture. Of course how you get to this point takes sketching shapes, erasing, reshaping, etc. Don't expect to just draw this perfect mannequin with your first strokes of pen or pencil.

Then add anatomy onto that structure.

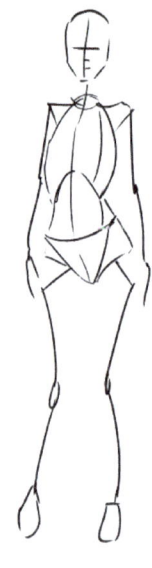 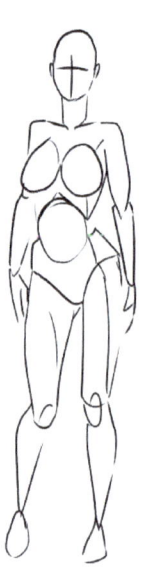 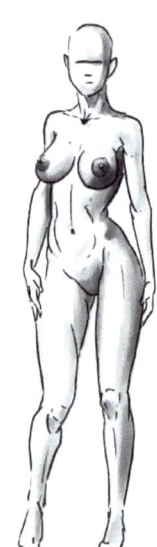

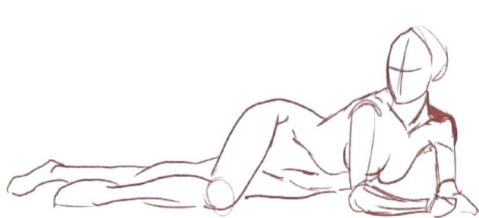 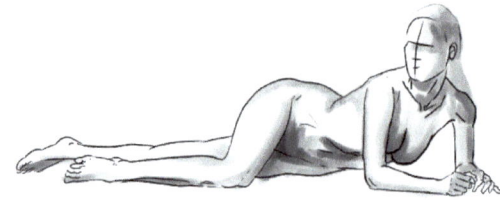

Be sure to keep gravity in mind. Watch where her thigh squishes into the ground. It changes the shape to be more flat.

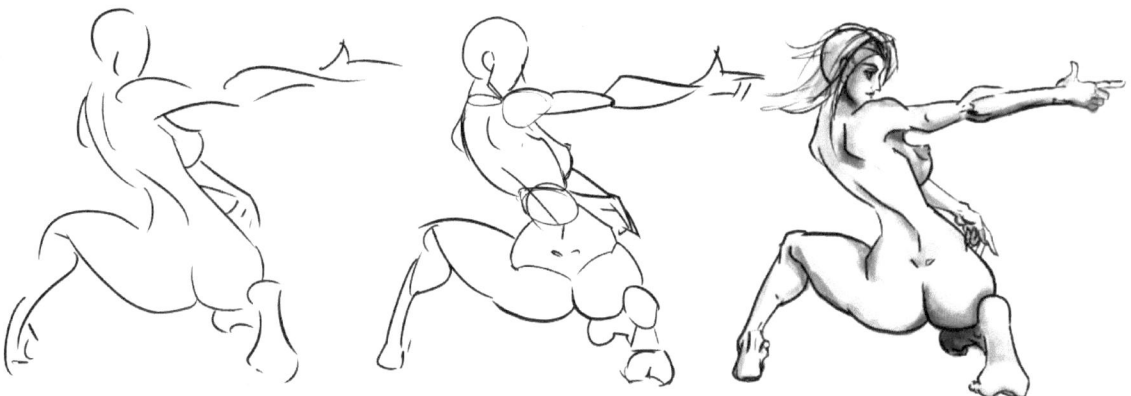

Sometimes I like to start with a gesture drawing because this really captures movement.

Once you find the structure, using the basic mannequin, you might lose some of the fluidity of the gesture, but that's okay.

As before, add in some anatomy. This time I kept it more stylistic.

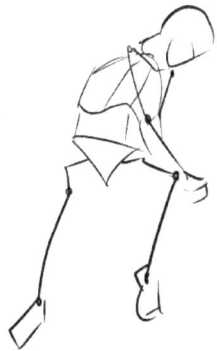

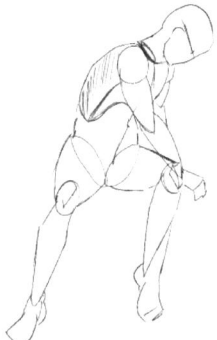

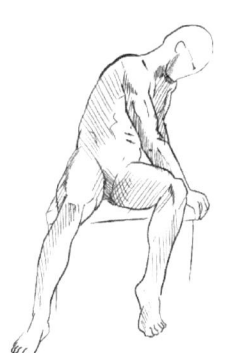

Sometimes a stick figure doesn't capture enough information to be useful to draw a pose. This is a good example.

Instead, I like to work the pose out with simple forms.

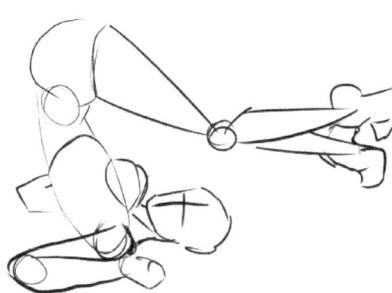

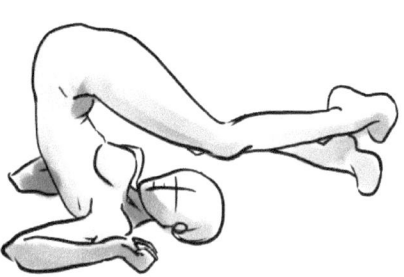

Using a stick figure for this femsale pose would be useless. Rather with many poses, you might find it easier to start with gesture or forms.

I changed the length of her torso before adding anatomy to my sketch.

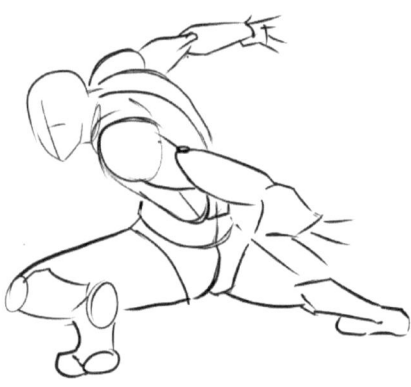
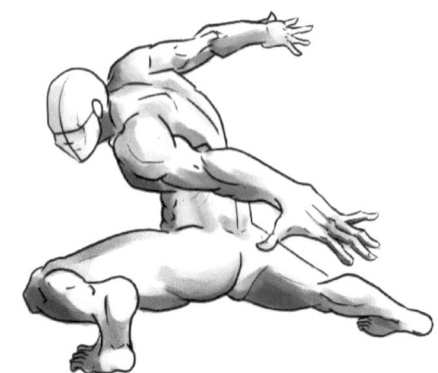

Poses like this can be a mind bender. Try to think of the basic shapes first. Keep in mind that you can see both the spine and the side view of the abs. You can see the butt in a 3/4 back view. Also, we have a good amount of foreshortening.

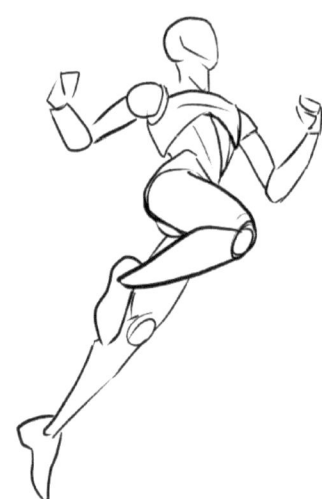
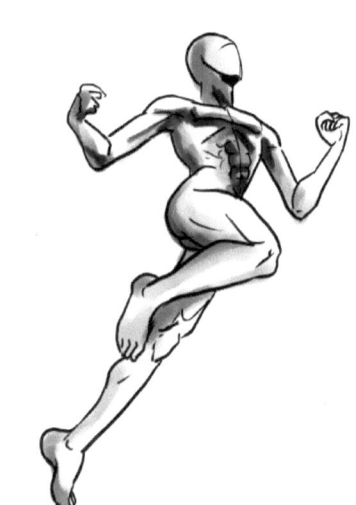

Remember when you are looking up at a figure teh shapes of pecks and such change.

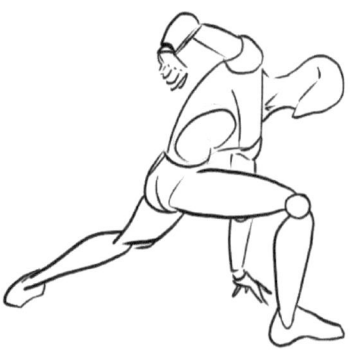
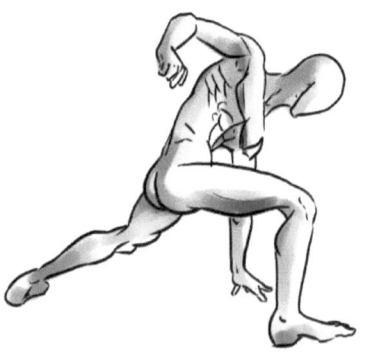

Chapter 8: Photo references

This chapter is a bonus chapter, offering many poses to study and draw from, all thanks to my girlfriend, who is wearing masking tape over her nipples and skin colored panties, so you don't have to worry about nudity.

Thank you to my girlfriend for sitting through this long photo session. It makes the book that much better.

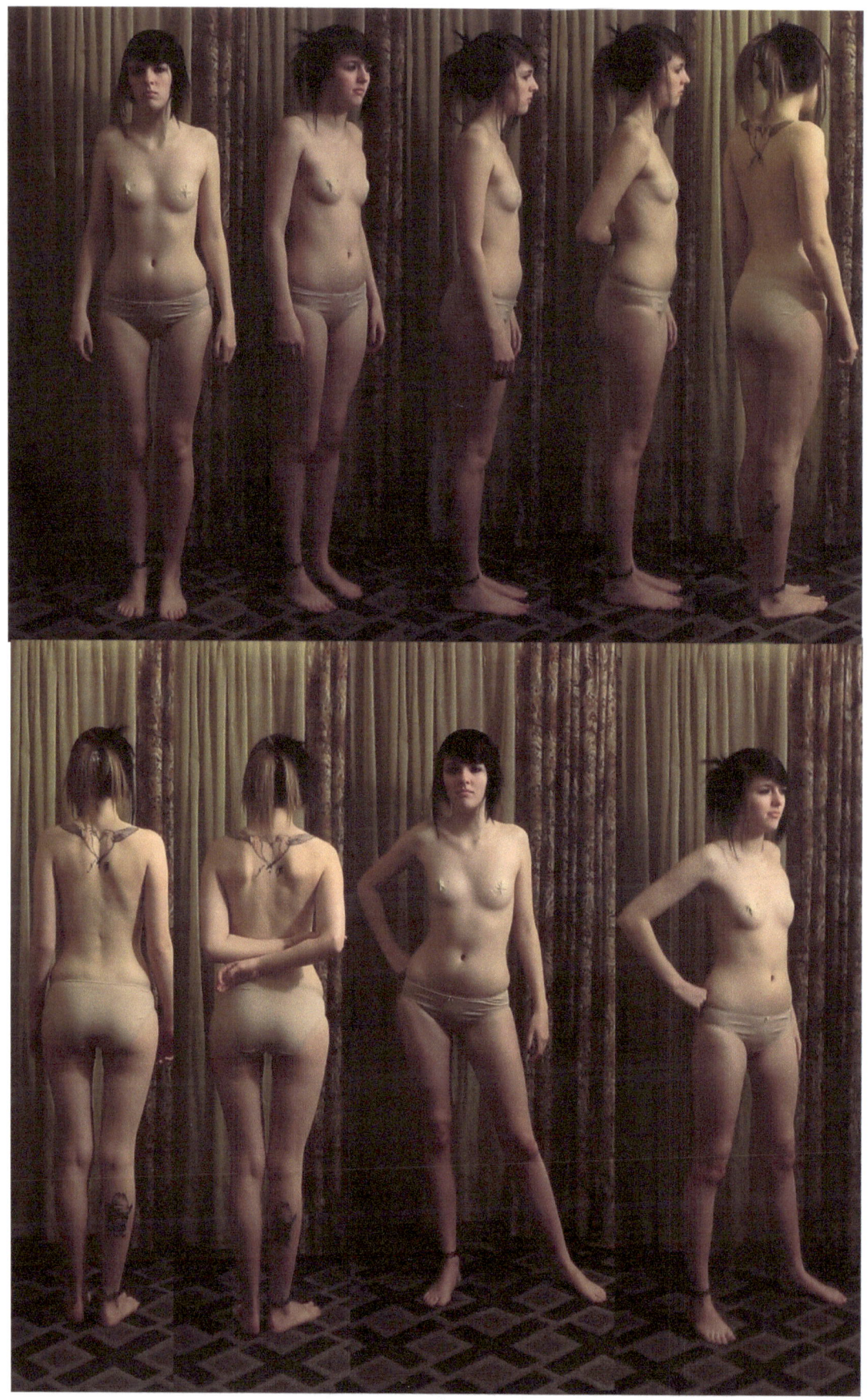

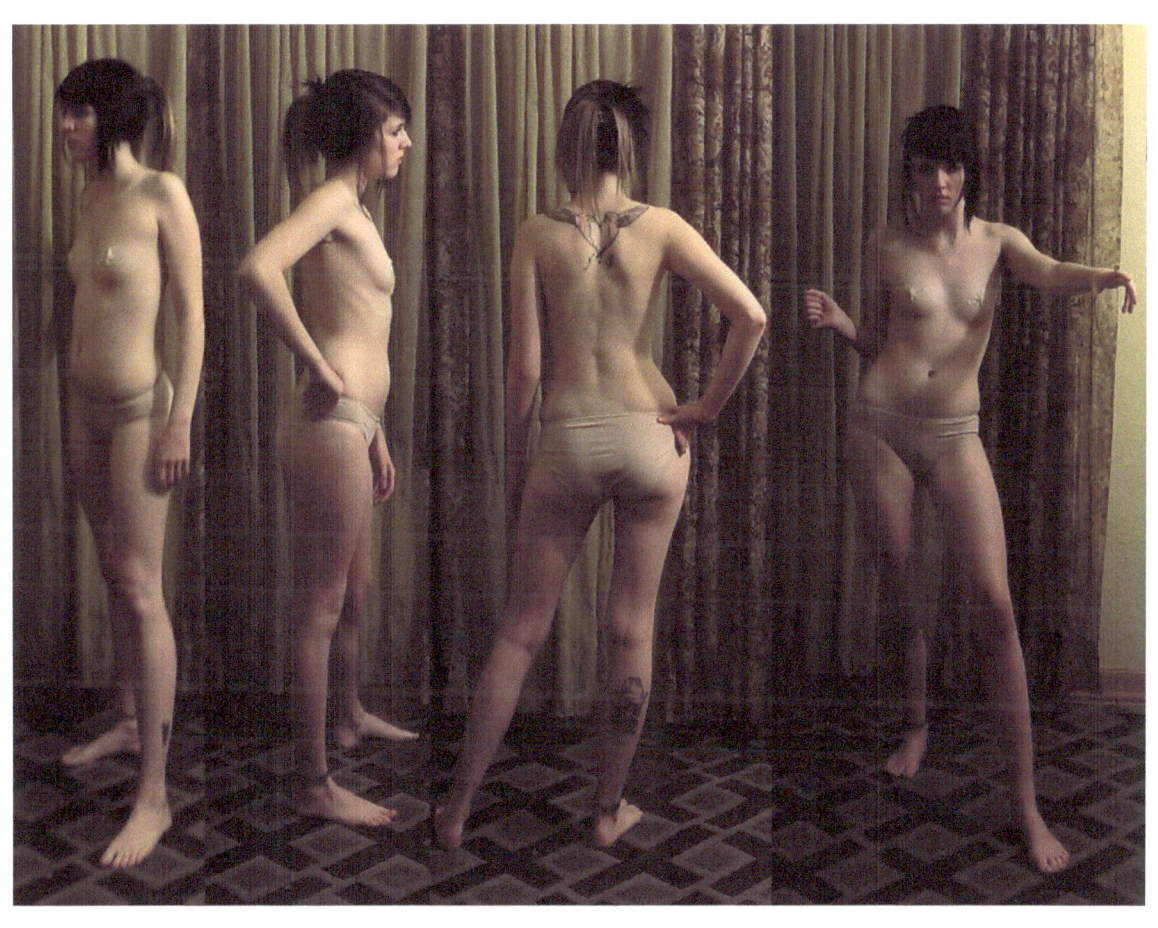
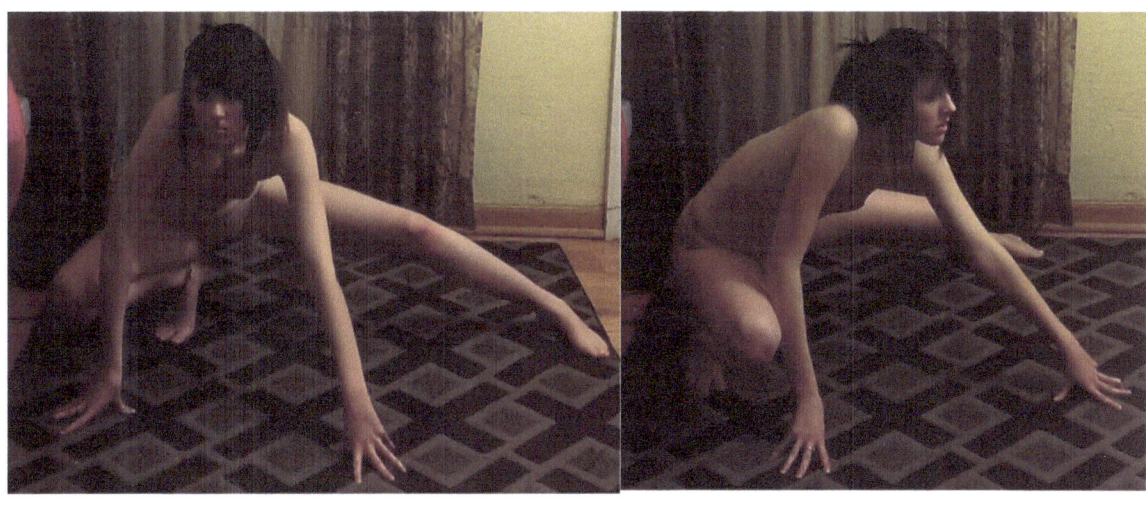

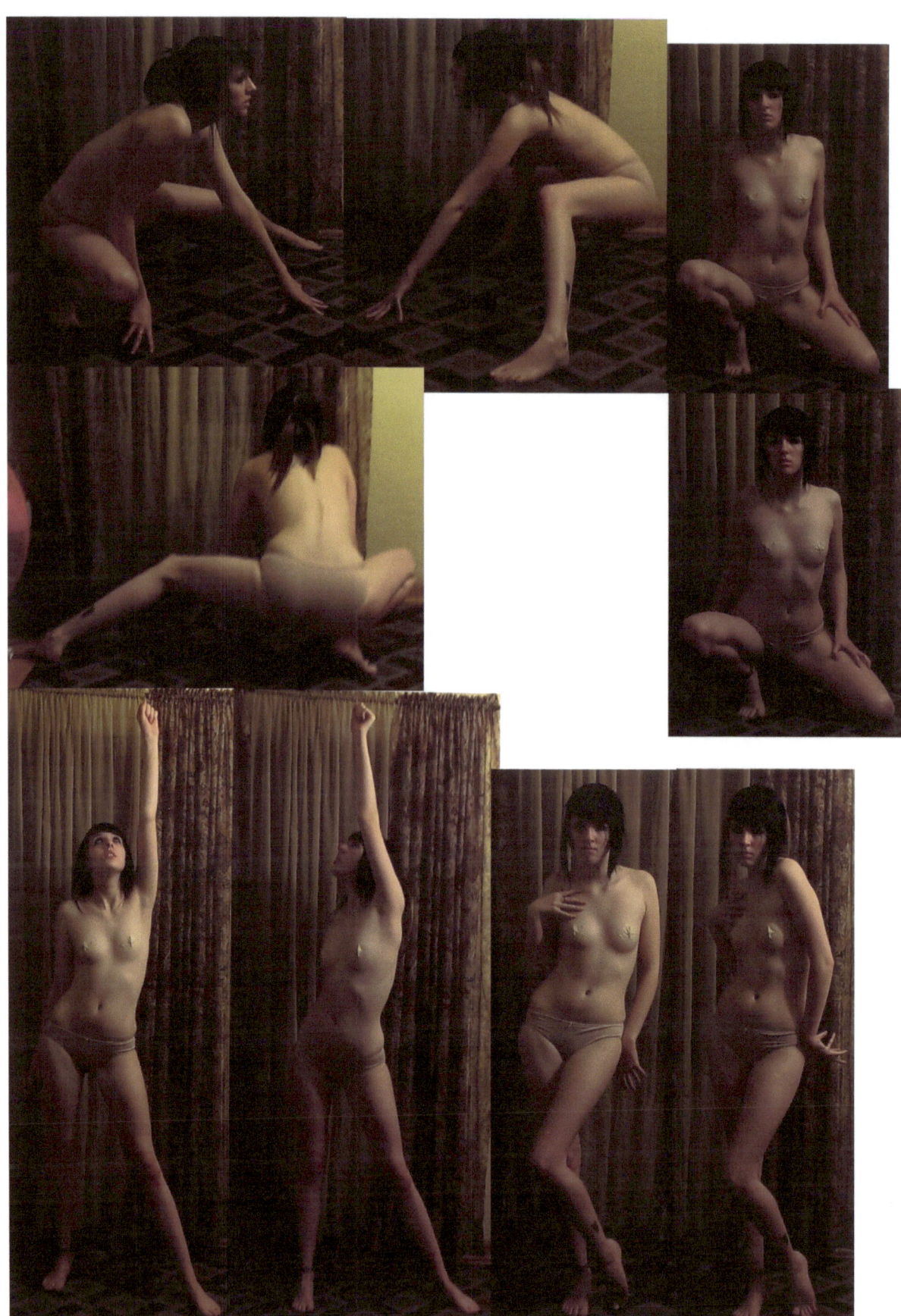

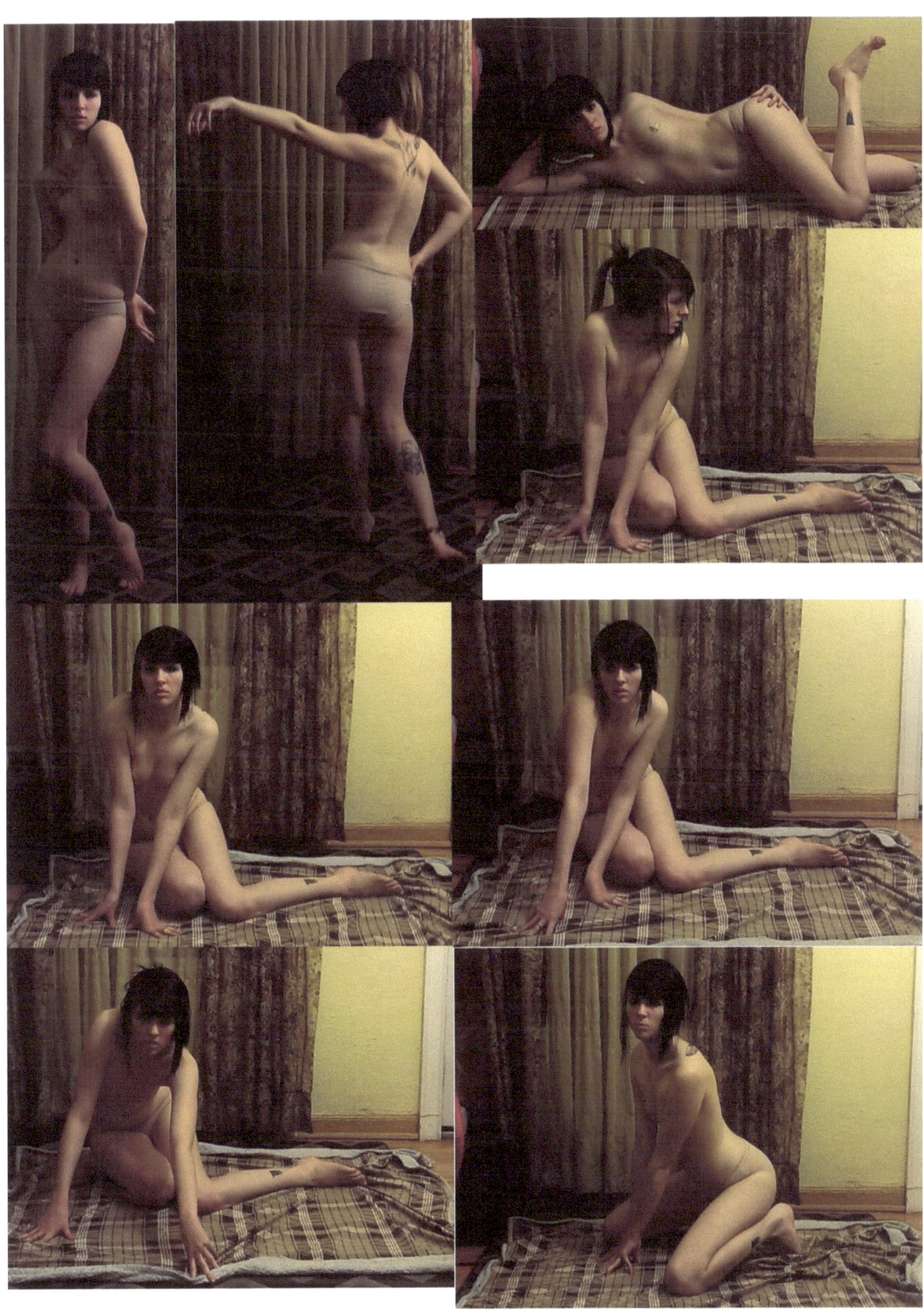

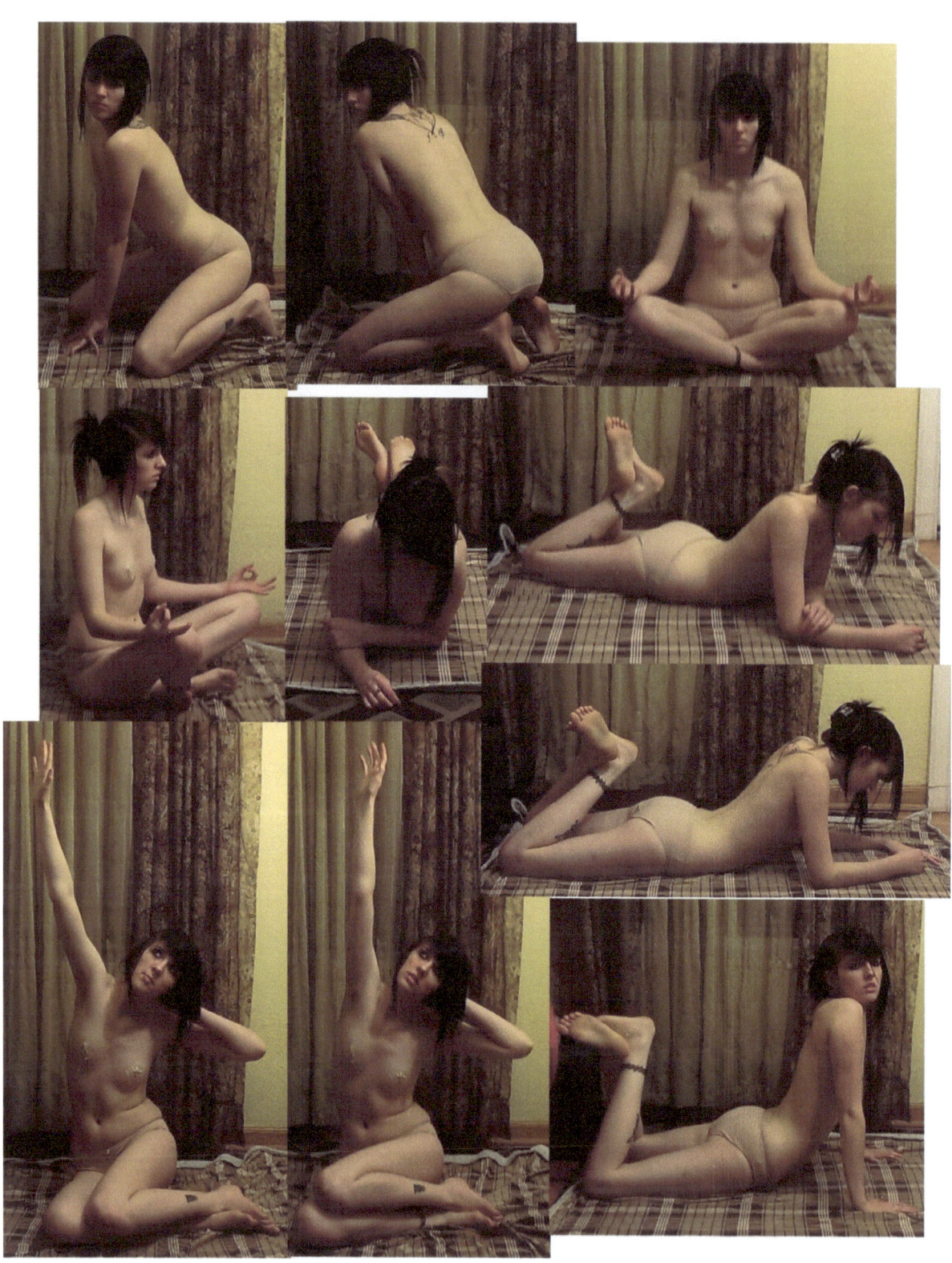

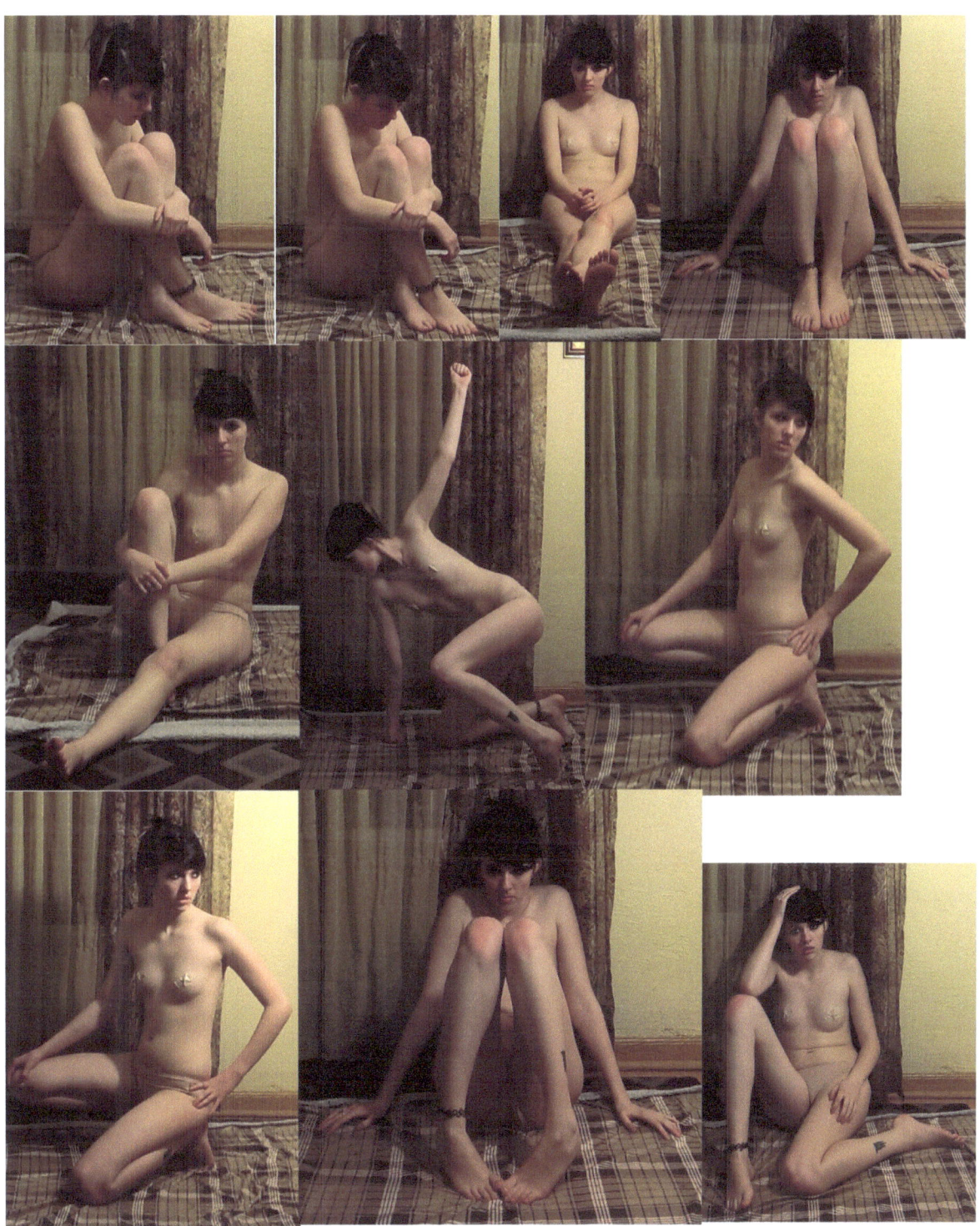

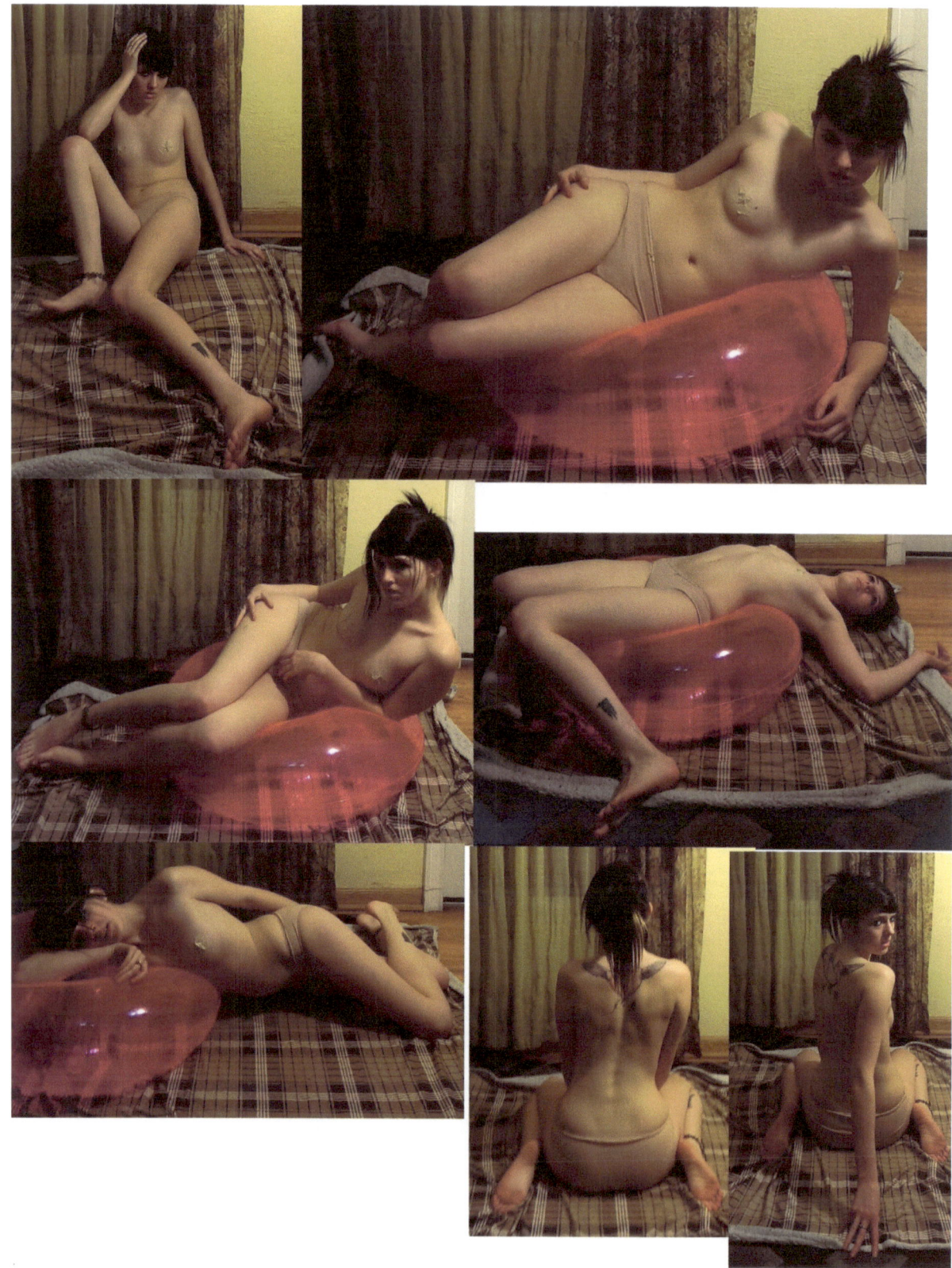

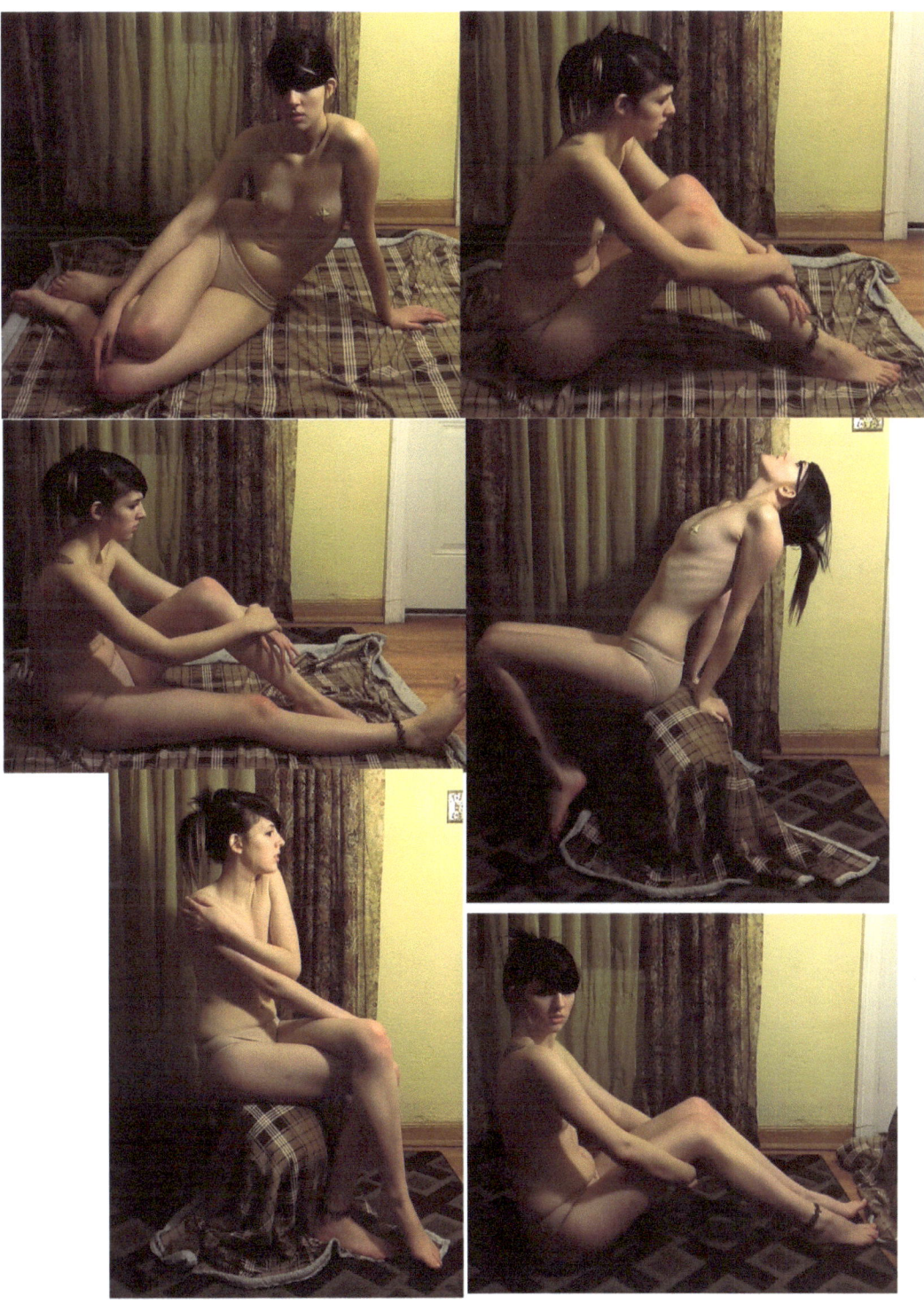

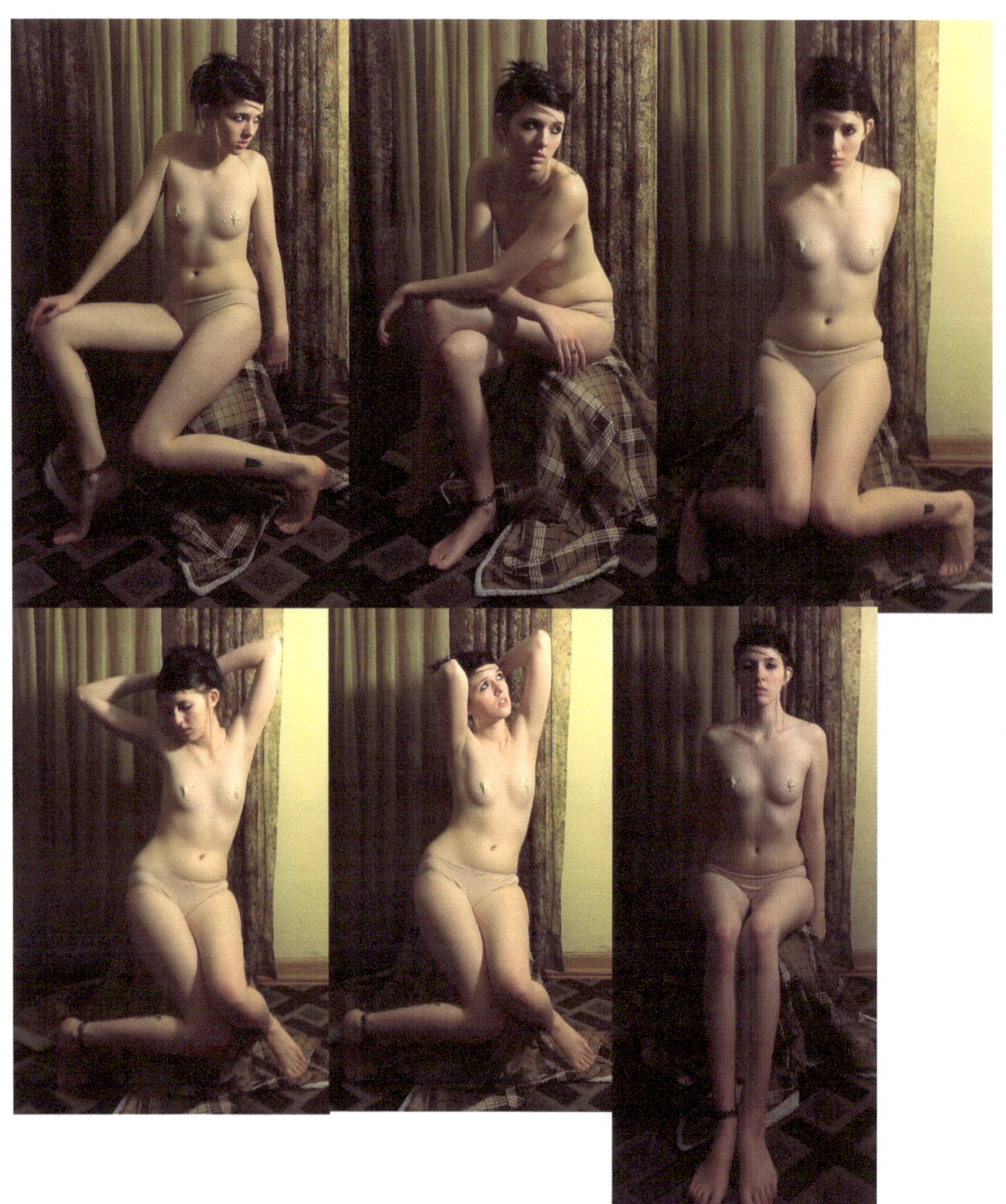

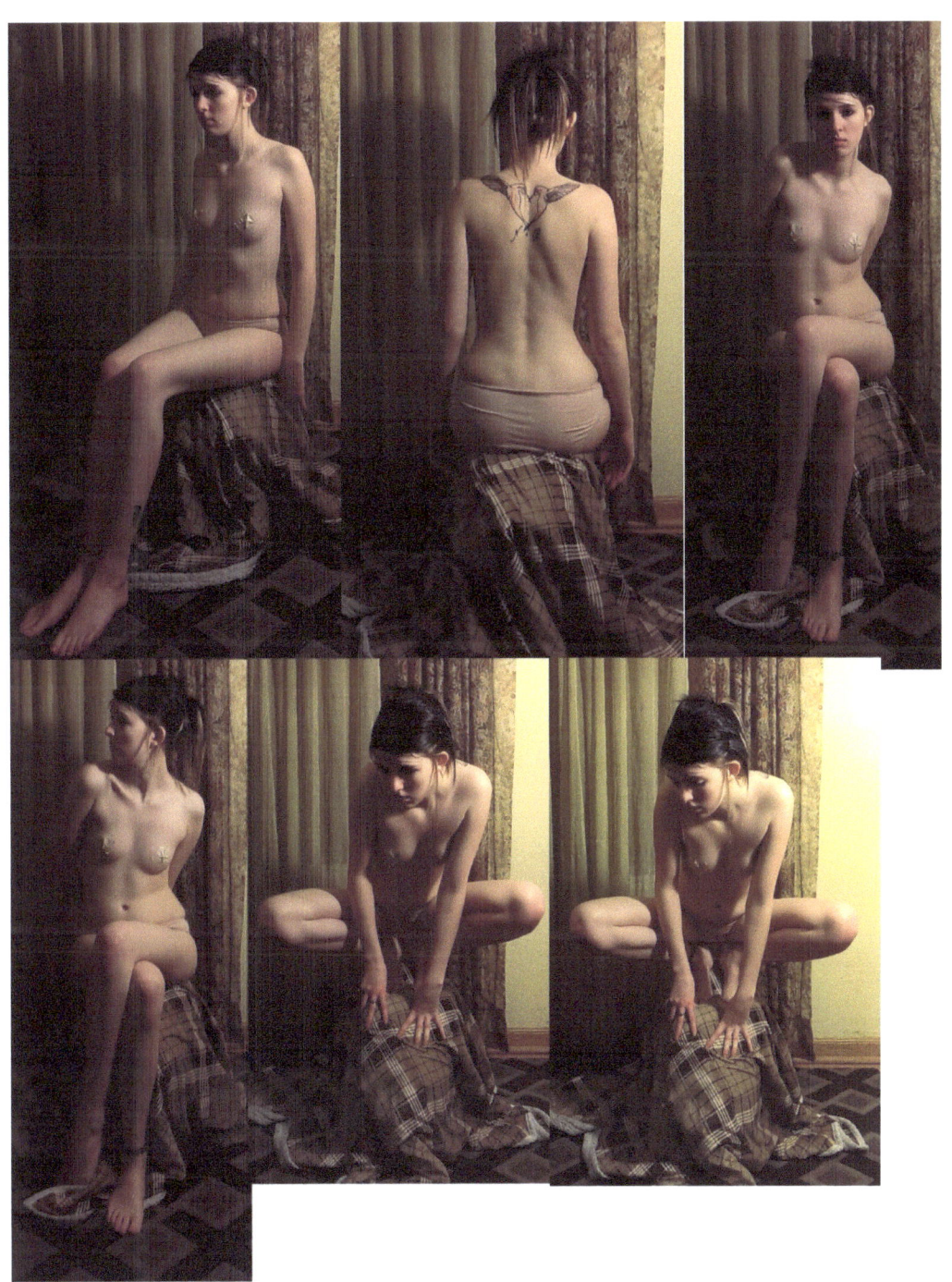

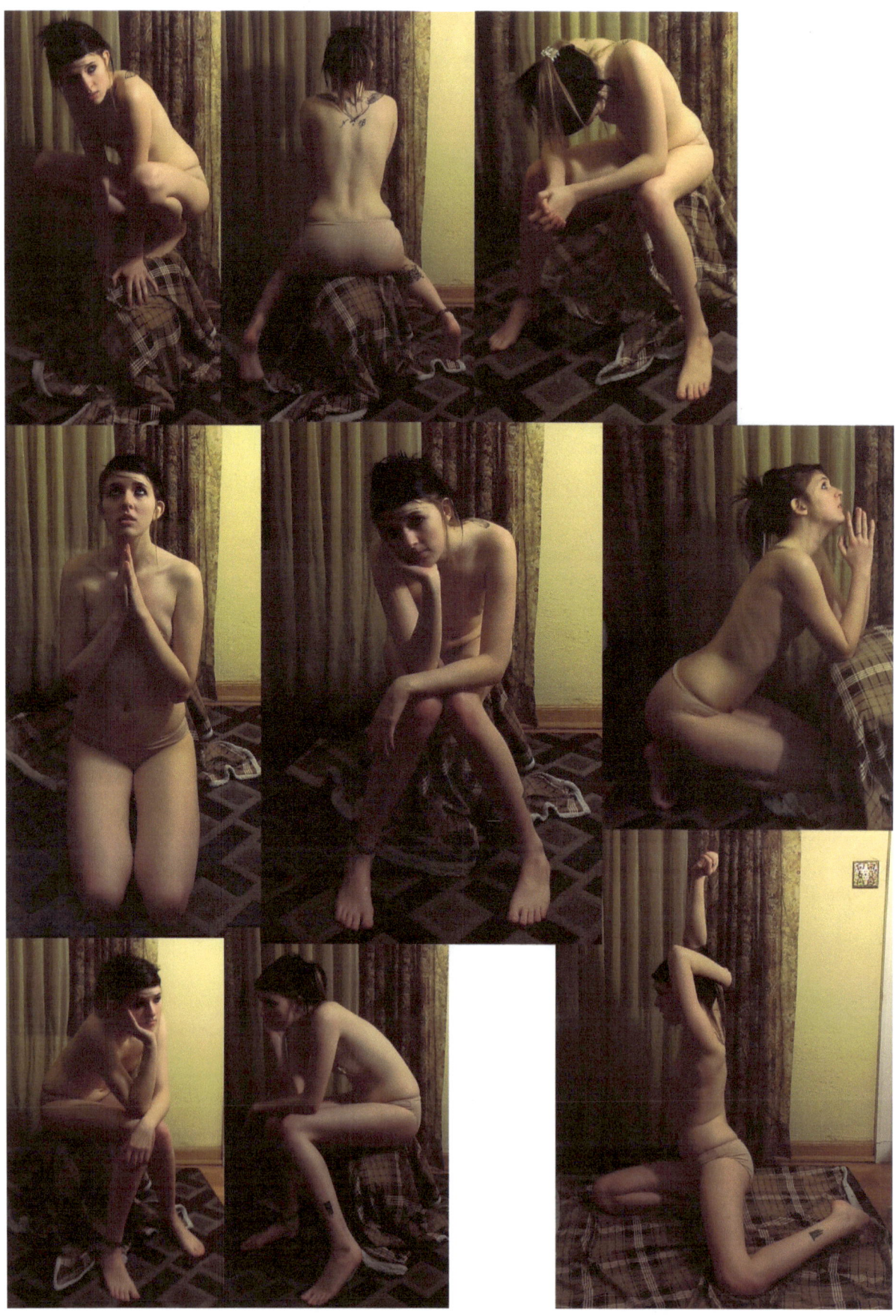

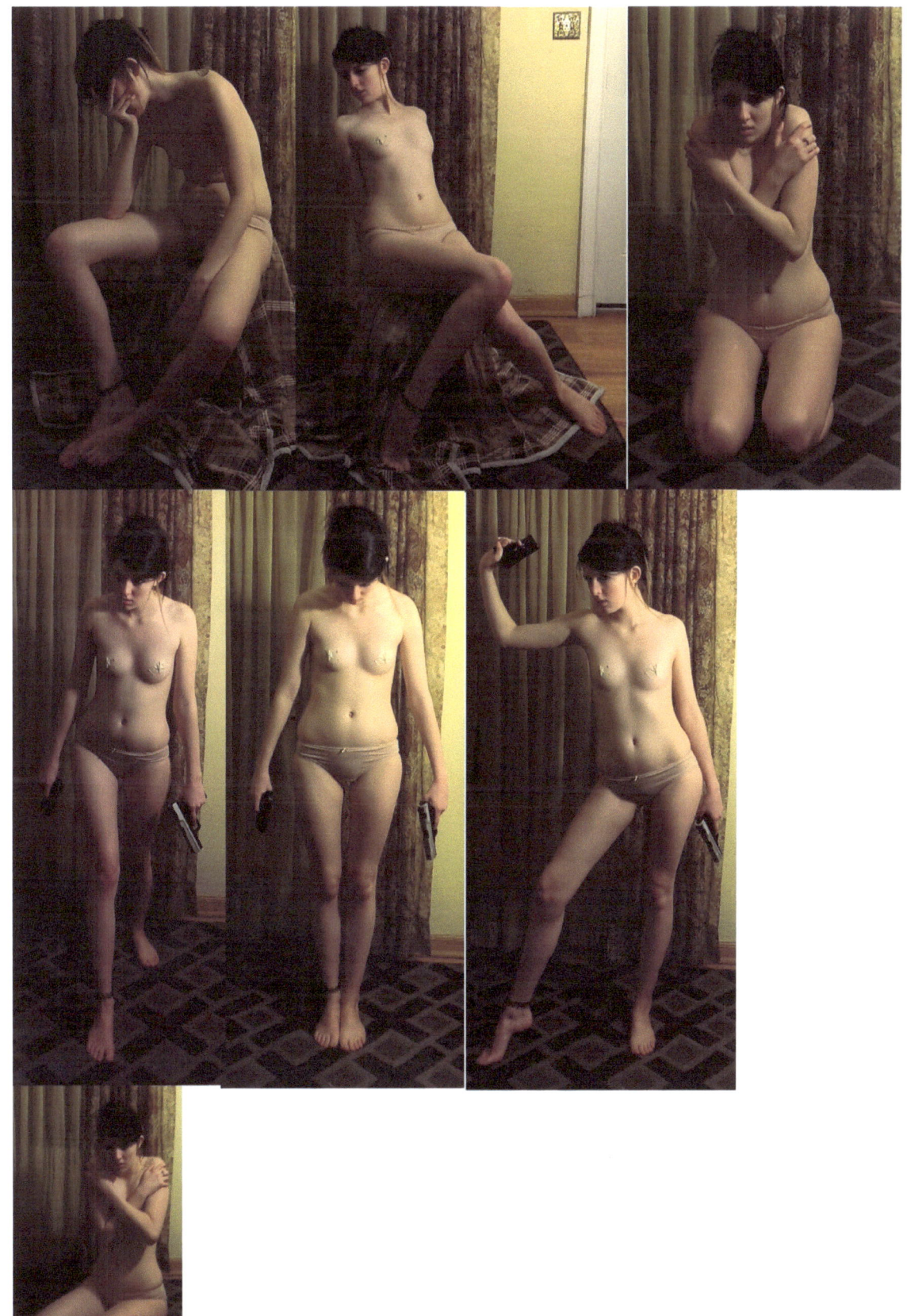

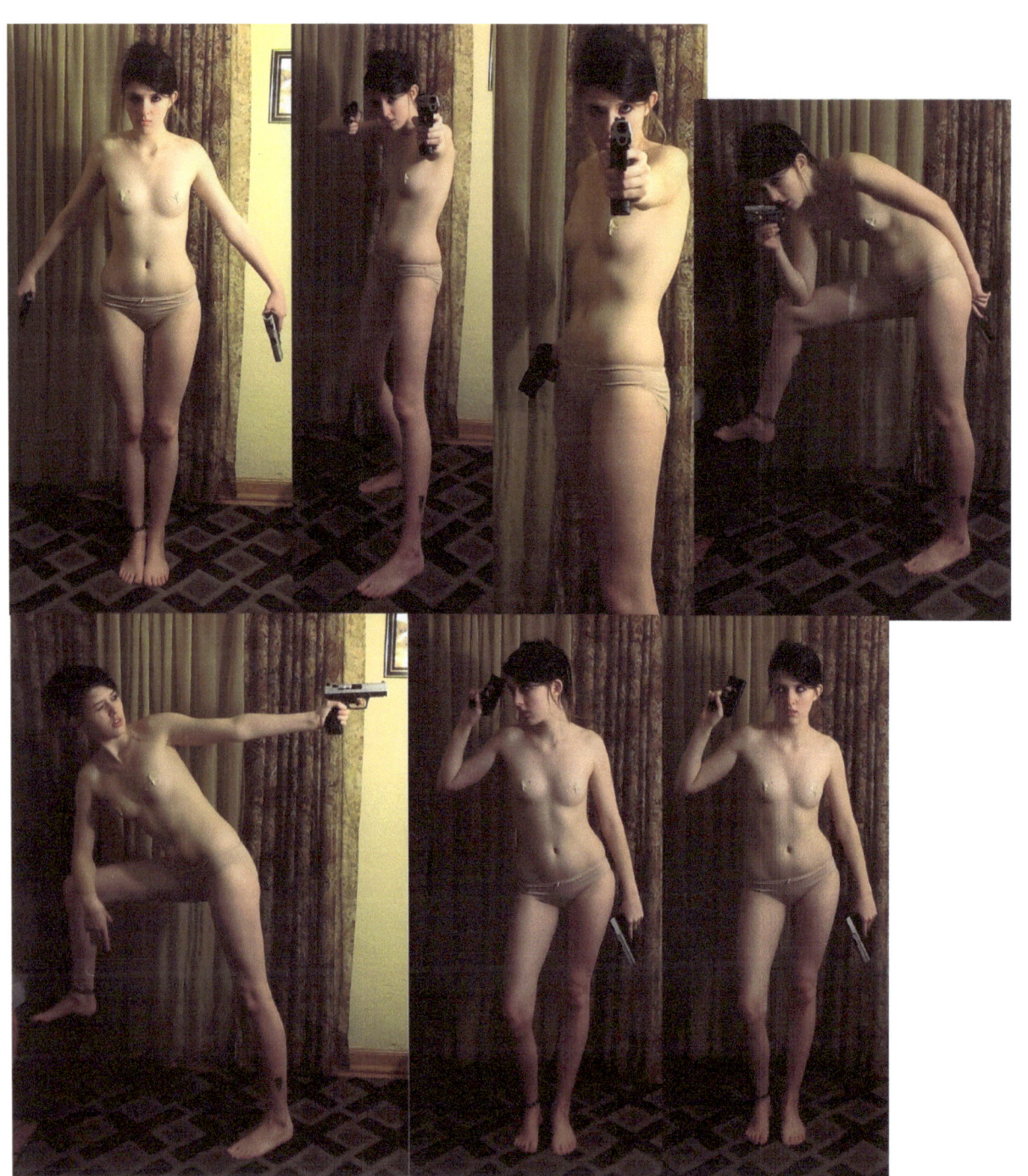

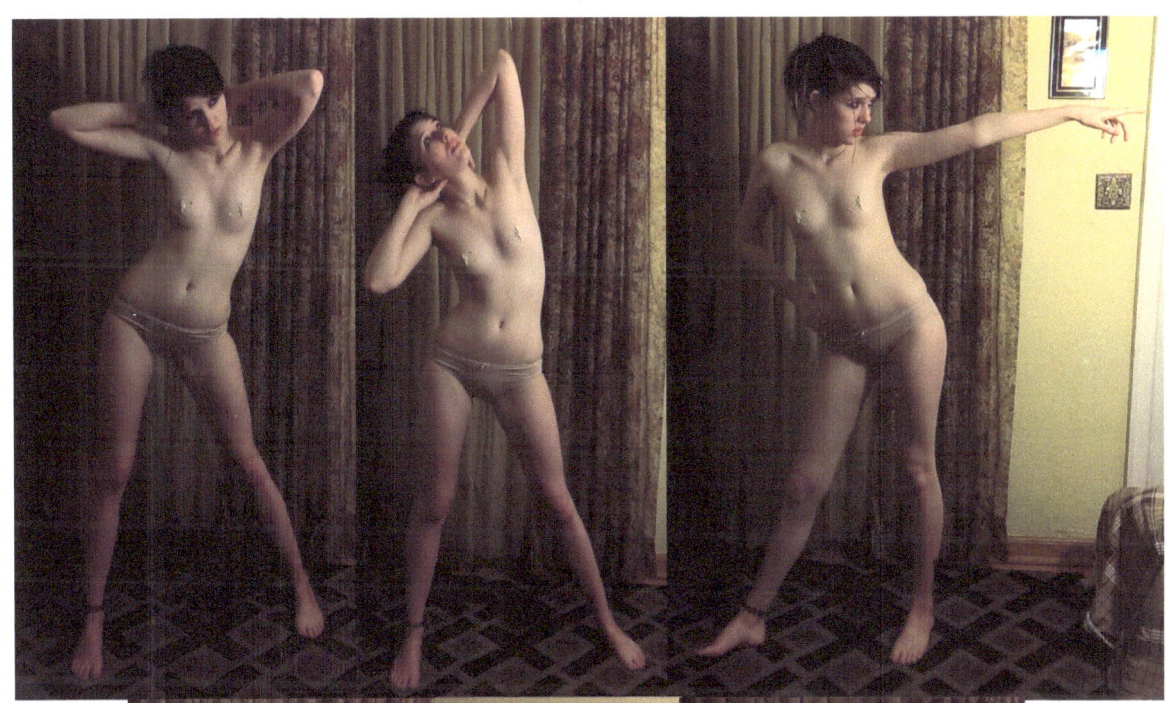
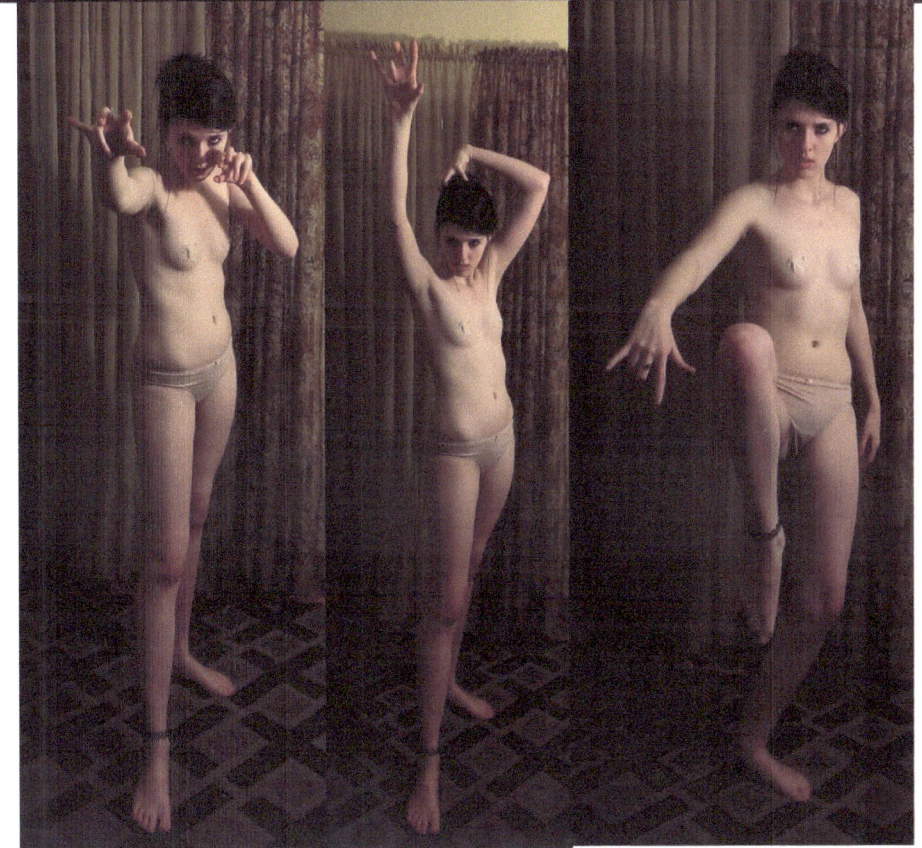

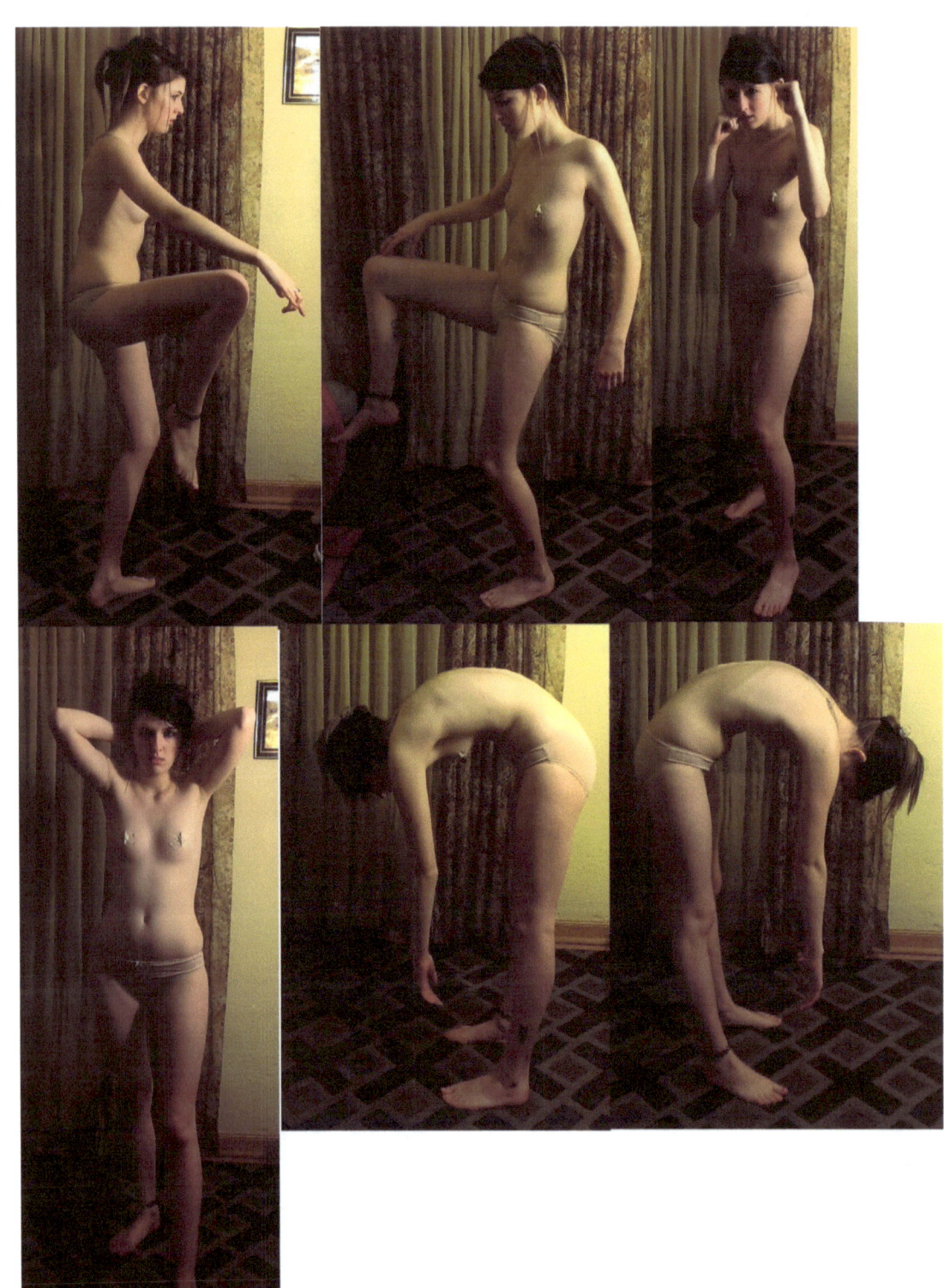

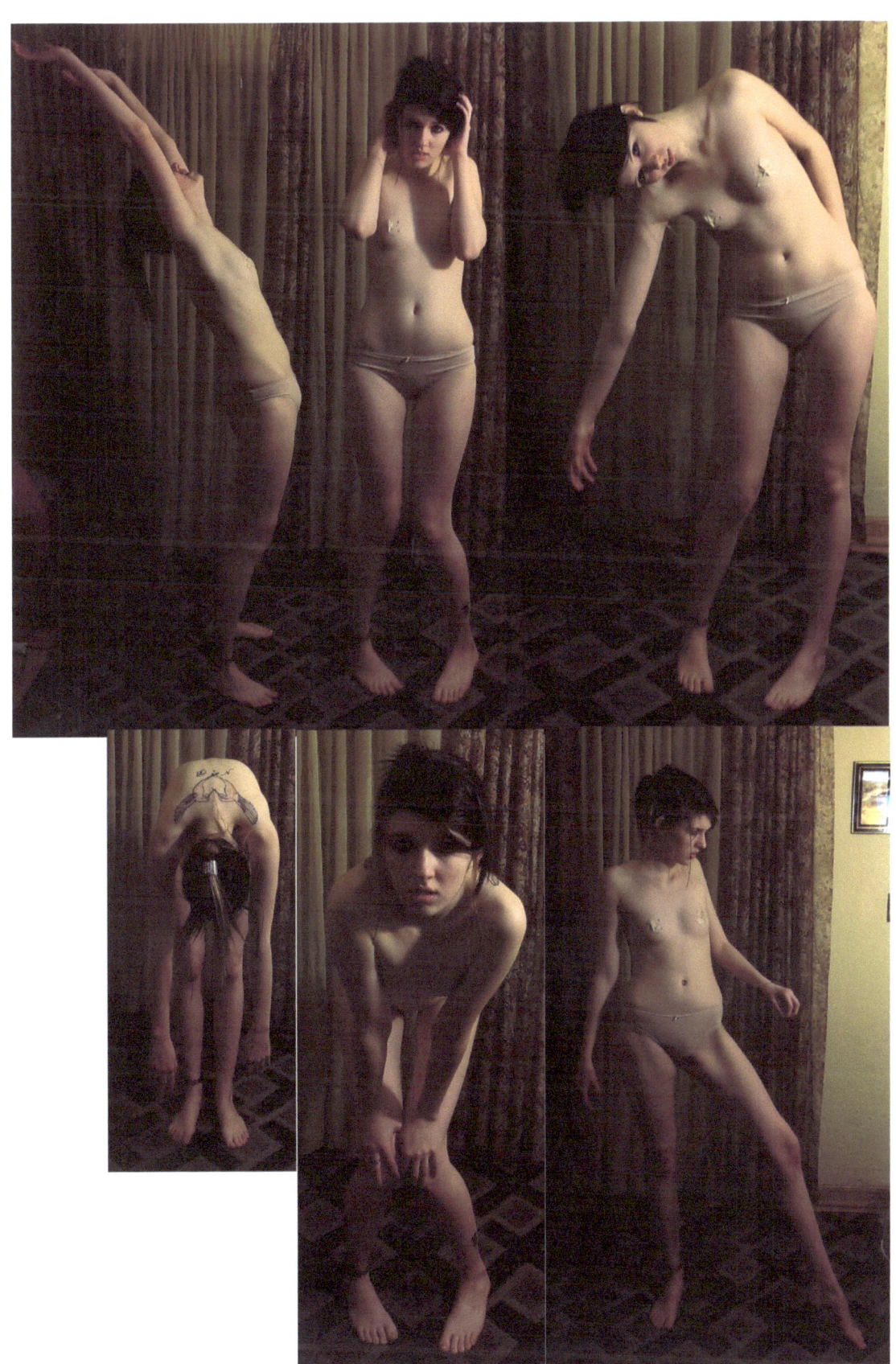

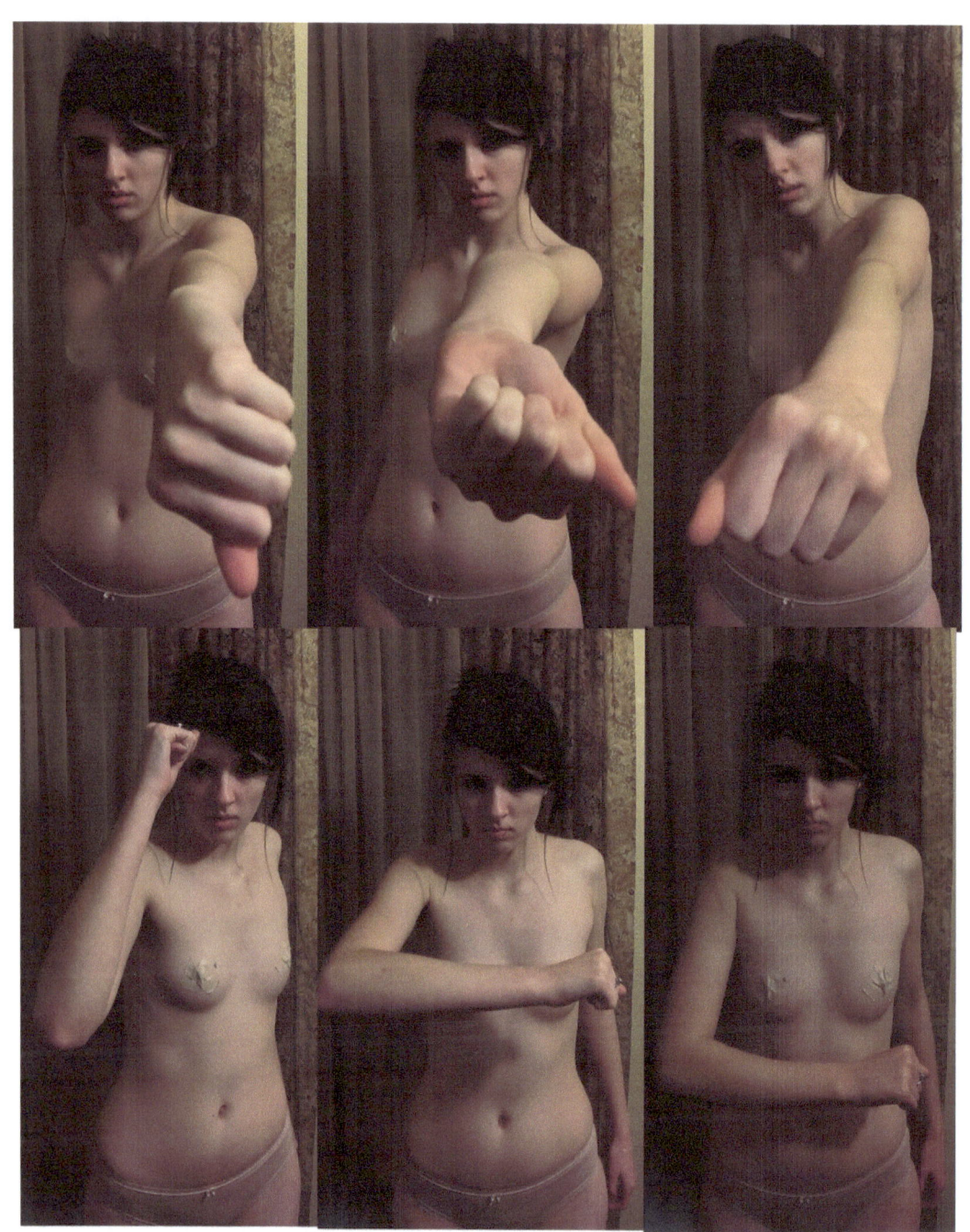

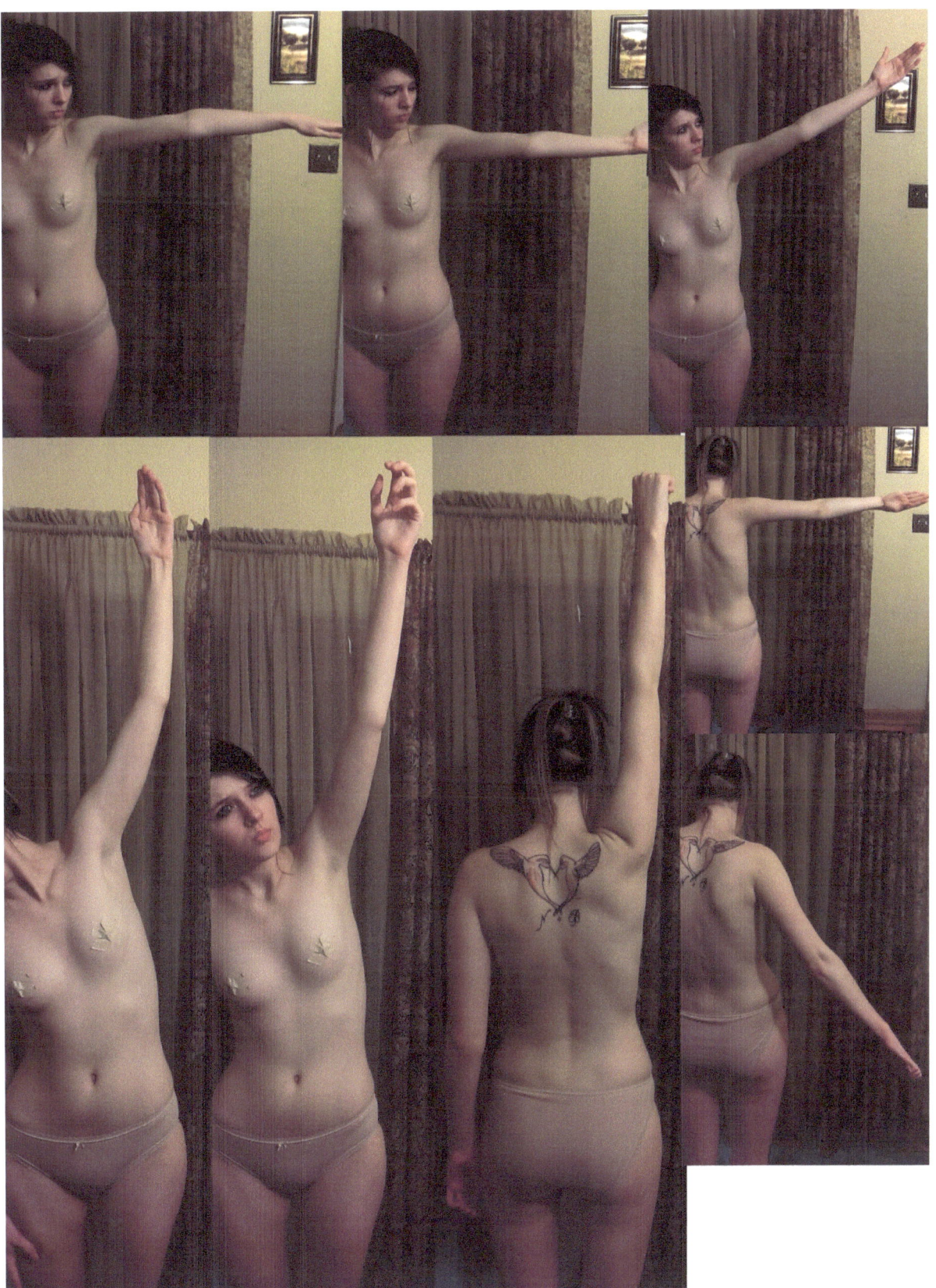

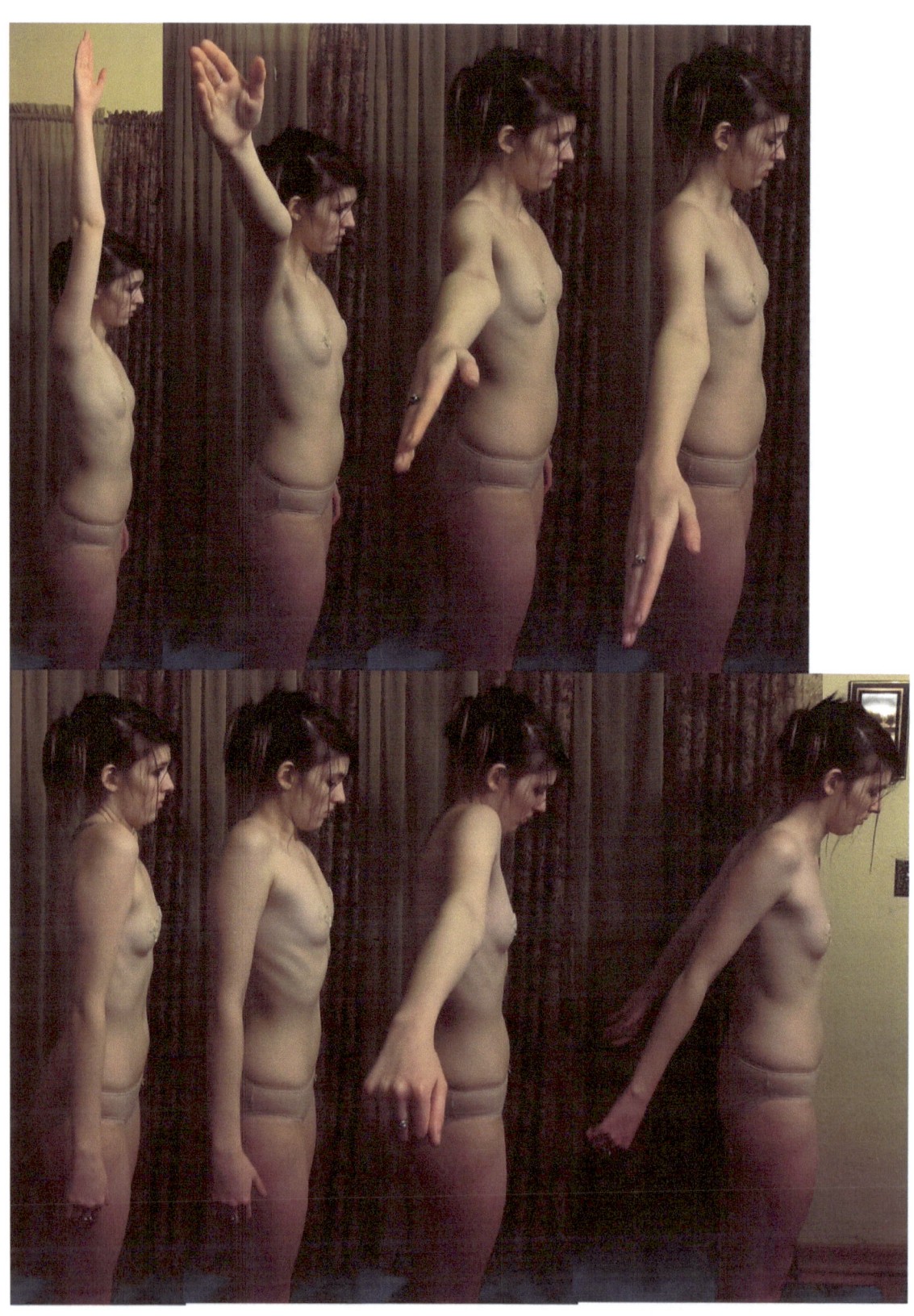

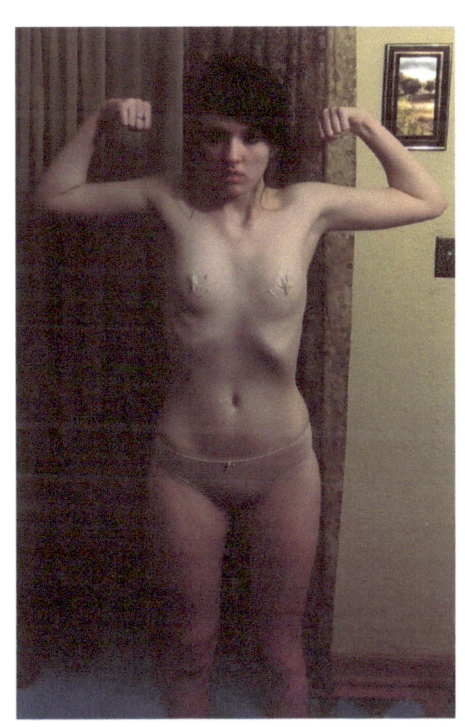

Notes

Thank you for purchasing this book. I am sure it has helped you draw better figures. However, I find it best to learn by video courses, so when you have the time, check out my video courses by going to http://masterpaintingnow.com

www.ingramcontent.com/pod-product-compliance
Lightning Source LLC
Chambersburg PA
CBHW050736180526
45159CB00003B/1251